GARDENS

IN THE MODERN LANDSCAPE

PENN STUDIES IN LANDSCAPE ARCHITECTURE

John Dixon Hunt, Series Editor

This series is dedicated to the study and promotion of a wide variety of approaches to landscape architecture, with special emphasis on connections between theory and practice. It includes monographs on key topics in history and theory, descriptions of projects by both established and rising designers, translations of major foreign-language texts, anthologies of theoretical and historical writings on classic issues, and critical writing by members of the profession of landscape architecture.

The series was the recipient of the Award of Honor in Communications from the American Society of Landscape Architects, 2006.

GARDENS
IN THE MODERN LANDSCAPE

A Facsimile of the Revised 1948 Edition

Christopher Tunnard

With a new foreword by John Dixon Hunt

PENN

University of Pennsylvania Press
Philadelphia

Published by
University of Pennsylvania Press
Philadelphia, Pennsylvania 19104-4112
www.upenn.edu/pennpress

Printed in the United States of America on acid-free paper
10 9 8 7 6 5 4 3 2 1

Library of Congress Cataloging-in-Publication Data
Tunnard, Christopher.
    Gardens in the modern landscape : a facsimile of the revised 1948 edition /
Christopher Tunnard ; with a new foreword by John Dixon Hunt. — 1st ed.
        p. cm. — (Penn studies in landscape architecture)
    Includes bibliographical references and index.
    Facsimile reprint. Originally published: New York : Scribner, 1948.
    ISBN 978-0-8122-2291-3 (pbk. : alk. paper)
    1. Gardens. 2. Landscape gardening. I. Title. II. Series: Penn studies in
landscape architecture.
SB472.T8 2014
712—dc23
                                                                                                      2014017083

CONTENTS

FOREWORD
to the Facsimile Edition

Gardens in the Modern Landscape, first published as a book in 1938 and again ten years later, is an important moment in discussions and promotions of modern gardens and landscape architecture. A foreword for this reprint requires two things: to situate the text, for those who come to it for the first time and even for those who know it (since Tunnard's writing emerges from a whole cluster of interrelated concerns); and, second, to assess how it survives today, both as a historical document and as an invitation to continue thinking about landscape architecture.

What is reprinted here is the second edition of 1948 (to which page references are given, unless otherwise stated). The changes made to the first are, in fact, modest. The wording of the text itself remains almost the same in both editions,[1] though the typeface is smaller and the images are now located in slightly different places on the page (so anyone citing pagination in these editions needs to specify which is being used). What gets altered textually in the second are mainly the substitution of a new and expanded "Foreword," the addition of a section on "Modern American Gardens" and, to conclude, an essay on "The Modern Garden" by Jospeh Hudnut, Dean of Harvard's Graduate School of Design, originally published in the *Bulletin* of the Garden Club of America.[2] Tunnard's original section on "The Oriental Aesthetics" is now merged with the section on "Asymmetrical Garden Planning" (and the subsection heading deleted), he expands the footnote on "Sharawadgi"[3] and inserts a new opening paragraph at the start of "A Solution for Today" (p. 143).

The Contents page of the 1948 book itemizes the different subsections of the chapters, not just their titles; "The Case for Community Gardens" in 1938 becomes simply "Community Gardens" in 1948. There is no change in the bibliography (though doubtless the wartime restrictions on paper made new publications less likely).

But image clusters are augmented, with some examples appearing in different places (the result, perhaps, of having to devise new signatures for a newly set text).[4] The plan of a garden arrangement by Garrett Eckbo at a Farm Security Administration camp in Texas is added on p. 142 in 1948, but with no commentary on it in the text. Some extra images are brought into the 1948 edition—notably a cluster of examples on "Architect's Plants" (pp. 118–25), which replaced the planting plans for Gaulby (1938, pp. 118–22), and others at the end of the section on "Art and Ornament" that illustrate modern interpretations of traditional forms. The biggest change is the dropping of a long final section on garden decoration for Grottoes, the Garden House, Gates & Fences, Garden Seats, Sculpture, and Conservancies (though two pages on "The Grotto" survived, now coming after "Reason and Romanticism" in 1948; a few of the other images from 1938 on garden decoration are used elsewhere in 1948[5]).

More interesting, I believe, is less the movement, such as it is, between the two editions and the juggling of image placement than the transference of Tunnard's original articles in the *Architectural Review* (*AR*), printed between October 1937 and September 1938, into a book published in late December 1938 by the Architectural Press, an in-house extension of the *Review*. While articles can stand alone, having a certain self-sufficiency that does not ask readers to situate them within a larger argument, once those same articles are gathered into a book (even if the texts are unaltered) they acquire and need a more consistent argument that moves between and sustains them. Illustrations, too, function differently in articles from their inclusion in books (even if the images are identical); new images and certainly the different placement of them in a fresh edition respond to a reading of the whole book, because its readers will be able to consult the entirety of images rather than just the ones attached to a single article; this again should make the whole more coherent than the individual parts as well as enlarge its concept and impact (indeed,

Tunnard does move clusters of images around in the two editions, perhaps to make a better impact; but he still allows many images in the book to do their own work, accompanied by captions but with no extended commentary in his main text).

Thus the transference of articles into a book does not always make for a coherent argument. While the 1948 edition, with Tunnard's self-criticisms and retractions, new additions, and the introduction of Hudnut's essay, is clearly something of an uneasy hold-all of rich and not always pursued ideas that Tunnard does not really do much about absorbing into a new structure, this is less true of the 1938 volume. Readers coming to it, especially without any sense that it emanated from a series of discrete articles and approaching it via the minimalist Contents page (which the 1948 edition would complicate with the insertions of many, not clearly adumbrated subheadings) will see the coherence. Even a reader like myself who has, as it were, done his homework can find 1938 a more sustained argument, and it is only our knowledge of Tunnard's new career in America after 1938 and the later version of 1948 that clouds our sense of what must have been, in 1938, an eloquent plea for modern gardens.

But the overriding issue throughout *Gardens in the Modern Landscape* (in both 1938 and 1948) and for its subsequent reception is surely Tunnard's understanding of modernist garden making and landscape architecture and his theoretical command of that material. This is in its turn allied to the dialogue between his garden practice and his ideas, for the practical work that he did in England largely petered out after he got to America in 1938 and certainly ceased when he moved to Yale as a regional planner in 1945.[6]

It is not easy to adjudicate his modernist stance, for a variety of good reasons. From the very beginning, he was exploring, finding his way in European modernism, and meshing what he found there with his involvement in his English practice and his theoretical ideas on English modernism. Then, too, he was trying to find a place for garden making in landscape architecture in modernist *architectural* theory, which was what he largely relied on, as well as in other competing concerns, such as his strong historical interest, community planning, and new housing. What also complicates these judgments is that Tunnard wrote the *AR* articles and published the book in England, while maintaining a freelance role, then promptly left to pursue a career in university teaching in America. Joining Harvard's GSD in 1938, he eventually (after a spell in the Canadian armed forces—he was a Canadian by birth) moved to Yale, where he established himself as an important regional designer and writer. These stops and changes don't make for a smooth intellectual trajectory, especially when you are—as was Tunnard—both curious and inquisitive and at the same time learning how to negotiate modernism in Europe and North America during a crucial period of both modernism itself and landscape architecture.[7]

People tended to judge Tunnard's book then (and still do nowadays) by where they locate him in his career—as a landscape architect or later as a planner—and/or the person who is writing about him—are they writing about him in England or America? The British journal *Landscape Design,* for example, said he had been "swamped by the American system"[8] (whatever *that* was supposed to be), and as late as 1989 Jane Brown's *Art and Architecture of English Gardens* wrote about his work from a wholly British perspective, which given his later career in planning might seem plausible as he seemed to have lost touch with garden art.[9] Many American landscape architects today, however, would consider his appeal to English landscape gardening of the late eighteenth century hopelessly irrelevant, and his continuing pleas for the lawn (albeit "in this country," i.e., Britain; see p. 67) offend large parts of the United States where chemicals are often used to keep grass immaculate and water is in short supply.

So we need to look at these different moments in his career as well as at its importance today. The main changes for the 1948 edition are crucial, but sit uneasily with the unchanged remainder of the 1938 text. The one and a quarter pages of the Foreword (pp. 5–6) in the first edition were short and straightforward. He argued that tradition and "experiment" are easily reconciled and that, given that the great ages of garden art were in Italy, France, and, by the eighteenth century, England, the "style for our own time … will not be very different from the humanized landscape tradition" of the latter. Since the nineteenth century had "debased all these traditions" to a "medley of styles," or maybe "formed the roots of the Modern movement . . . now developing," and since many eighteenth-century garden landscapes were "disappearing," the need was to create a new landscape for the twentieth century. This seemed to imply that a "style for our time" necessitated an emphasis on planning and a focus on "houses, factories, shops and places of amusement . . . the street, the park and the rationally-planned community" (1938, p. 5). He ended with the confidence that a clearer picture of what a garden is, or should be, would emerge to satisfy the "complex needs of modern society." The language is generalized, even for a Foreword: "style," a term he often used in the rest of the work, does not begin to explain how the usage of this term can appeal to "today."

The four-page 1948 Foreword is more embattled and also a little defensive. He begins by addressing the "conclusions" that have been reached in the intervening ten years, though many people have been engaged in "other occupations" (the war, but perhaps his own move to America and toward planning). He continues to insist that eighteenth-century English landscaping was right and admired its transference to North America; that its emphasis on locality, on observing "genius of place," was still necessary. He back-tracks slightly on his distaste for nineteenth-century garden art, saying now that it was not all "mere essays in copyism" but productive of new forms and expressions. His attitude toward modernism has also changed as a result of "seeing more examples"—an "accumulation of acquired knowledge" certainly trumps "intuitiveness"! Citing a "manifesto" that he says he authored jointly with Jean Canneel-Claes,[10] he now acknowledges that he would himself need to modify their original claim that past "philosophy" or landscape "origins" can be ignored (this modification thus resisting out-and-out "modernism"). He cites an American professor who wanted "less history and more modern things" in Tunnard's next book, and he rebuts it by quoting Geoffrey Scott. Hence, his renewed call for "pleasing variety" in design that allows him to insist again on Sharawadgi. Finally, he refuses to accept that architects and planners can "help to build a better society"; they "must," however (and this seems muddled), go into community planning, because, while they may shape a plan, "they should not try to dictate its final *form*" (my italics). He then denigrates (p. 7) the work of a host of technocrats, of anti-intellectualism and organic plantsmanship. His own skills must honor usefulness, aesthetic qualities, good materials, and the wishes of the client.

The three ideas he expounds in the pages that follow in the center of the book have to do with functionalism, empathy, and aesthetics. He discusses the first in "Towards a New Technique" (pp. 69–80), the second while exploring Japanese garden art under the rubric of asymmetrical garden planning (pp. 81–92), and the third in the section "Art and Ornament" (pp. 93–98). His emphasis upon functionalism espouses simplicity and an un-Victorian and Edwardian sparseness and insists on its fitness for the purpose envisaged and sees the obvious need to ensure that garden design responds to contemporary activities (tennis and swimming pools, not croquet lawns) as well as "traditional elements." The oriental legacy had introduced "asymetrical garden planning" into the eighteenth century, and what modern design now needs is to seize an "occult" balance—an "interplay of background and foreground, height and depth, motion and rest"—that is exemplified by the "spiritual quality in inanimate objects" that Tunnard finds in Japan; it is this "unity of the habitation within its environment" that elicits one of Tunnard's more eloquent and thoughtful meditations on how we might connect with a garden's forms.

On aesthetics, he first begins by deleting a section on beauty,[11] presumably because he now suspects its analogy is awkward, as if bread cannot be *both* nourishing and pleasing and as if bread and gardens have the same function. But he continues to insist, as he did in the very first paragraph of his book, that the garden is like "an aesthetic composition" that needs to be maintained in the face of a naturalistic confusion that gardens ought to imitate nature. This confusion he attributes to the fuzzy thinking on the part of amateur English gentlemen and ladies who think of landscaping as a "hobby" (p. 11). While he agrees that it is hard to accept that the garden *is* a work of art and needs to be seen as a mediated activity, he proposes that the best of modern sculpture can be invoked to rethink garden ornament: both *objets trouvés* and the ancient stones and monoliths of ancient Britain (which can somehow be referenced in those objects). These were of especial interest to Paul Nash, who provided Tunnard with a photograph of standing stones in Cornwall[12] and one of whose "objects" was illustrated and discussed (pp. 95 and 100). Tunnard argued that a garden designer needed to "co-operate with Nature" rather than "becoming a slave to her demands" (p. 95). The modern designer cannot be "bound by the conventional necessity for picturesque representation, and looks upon the imitation of Nature as a long-perpetuated artistic fraud" (p. 80). We may sense here a need that recalls the earliest historical objections to "Capability" Brown's work that it seemed no different from common fields and allies it with an ecological fundamentalism: landscape architecture should look like landscape architecture and be, in some way, distinguishable from what surrounds it that is not.

It would be hard to see Tunnard as a theoretician.[13] His own education in Europe had a touch of Autolycus in *A Winter's Tale*, a "snapper-up of unconsidered trifles." Yet what he gathered was not unconsidered, only piecemeal. He garnered ideas on Japanese gardens from Percy S. Cane, for whom he worked between 1932 and 1935, but he may also have seen Japanese examples in his early years growing up in California.[14] He also admired the work of the potter Bernard Leach, who had studied in Japan and returned to practice in Cornwall with a Japanese potter.[15] He learned much when he visited Paris for a congress arranged by the Société Française des Architectes de Jardins, which occurred at the same time as the Exposition Internationale des Arts et Techniques dans la Vie Moderne, which also showed garden designs by André and Paul Vera.[16] In Paris he encountered Achille Duchêne, the "re-inventor" of classical seventeenth-century French gardens for the present day; the Swedish Sven A. Hermelin, "who espoused functionalism and free planning";[17] the Belgian Jean Canneel-Claes, one of whose designs was featured in 1938 (pp. 64–65) and again in 1948 (p. 65); and other designers such as Gabriel Guevrekian. He maybe borrowed a term like "architectural plants" from the Swiss M. Correvon's coinage of plants as "formes architecturales,"[18] and introduced a set of a dozen images of such plants to support this. In England he was well connected with and worked for architects such as Raymond McGrath, Serge Chermayeff, A. J. Powell, and Oliver Hill.[19] He probably derived most stimulation from his membership in MARS (Modern Architectural Research Group), which argued for housing and a functional social agenda; MARS was the British arm of the Congrès International d'Architecture Moderne (CIAM). But he also knew artists such as Henry Moore, Ben Nicholson, John Piper, Barbara Hepworth, Naum Gabo, and especially Paul Nash, whose garden he and Frank Clark designed.[20] Nash's well-mannered surrealism may also have attracted him: in Tunnard's design for Bentley Wood, a noticeable feature is the open screen at the end of the patio, through whose ten rectangular openings we see the parkland beyond (published as the frontispiece in 1938 but in 1948 on p. 68). This is a familiar and repeated device in Paul Nash's paintings, such as *Landscape from a Dream* (1936–38), another *Landscape from a Dream* (1936–38), and *Month of March* (1929).[21] He also liked and used draughtsmen such as Gordon Cullen—his own graphic skills were not very good—whose lines and almost cartoon-like skill gave his projects a recognizable modernist effect. This graphic style, sharp and abstract like that of other earlier modernist designers in France such as Jean-Claude Nicolas Forestier, Pierre-Émile Legrain, and the Vera brothers, did suggest a much less traditional way of *representing* garden art, and it is curious how with all those designers we are more used to seeing their graphic rather than their finished work.

Tunnard's own designs, both built and drawn (by others), suggest his strong desire to find a modernist "style," if not always a modernist function. But "style" seems an awkward term, too often used in architectural writing when talking of a particular period or designer in ways that detract from its cultural content. Interestingly, he drops from the 1948 edition examples of different "styles" of garden elements, such as chairs and benches (1938, pp. 166–82), that implied too superficially that style was what determined a modern garden. He himself pillories it by citing Le Corbusier (p. 71)—"The styles are a lie"—who goes on to argue that in any epoch, "style" is what can be understood to unify and animate what is built. Landscape (as well as buildings) should not be labeled with this or that style but should address "site, enclosure, and materials" as a complex and intertwined whole.[22] The permanence of any "architectural [sc. landscape] topic results from its essential *correspondence* with a recurring and fundamental human condition." These conditions may change, but they will recur, and their recurrence necessitates that we reexamine contemporary sites by envisaging how they are enclosed, how they respond to current demands and expectations, and how they utilize available materials. All that involves an adequate and exciting "correspondence" between new experience and long-standing practice: this allows, as Tunnard wrote in the 1938 Foreword, that tradition and experiment be reconciled. And Holmes Perkins annotated his copy of Tunnard's 1938 edition with two phrases: "all gardens = adaptations of past interventions" and "no tabula rasa."[23] Tunnard himself, too, assures his readers (p. 67) that "a new garden technique ... need not necessarily reject the traditional elements of the garden plan." Now this, despite Tunnard's reliance upon the term "style," is what he attends to more often than not when he looks to that triad of materials, site, and enclosure. He sees the need to relate gardens to the site and especially its house, and he notes how little idea of the "whole design" (p. 18) is visible in "villa gardens" today (p. 24). But he also envisages gardens that have both finite and permeable boundaries, and he explores on several occasions how gardens situate their spaces within larger landscapes. He notes the "necessity" of using new materials from plant importation and hybridization and their methods of application (p. 62), yet (somewhat ambiguously) sees "the rise of scientific horticulture [as] the partial eclipse of garden planning" (p. 63), not least in an ecological refusal to use natural materials in unusual ways.

One problem with the modern(ist) garden is that the forms of garden elements are still hugely atavistic (as Tunnard himself makes clear); garden plants willfully continue to behave as plants (however artists drew them). He much disliked arts and craft gardens, because he and perhaps Frank Clark, who collaborated with him on several planting designs, found Gertrude Jekyll's reliance on impressionist planting dated; yet he was less able or certain how to utilize plant materials within sites that he could treat with more modern forms, and he withdrew from the second edition his planting plans for the areas around the new house at Gaulby (1938, pp. 119–22), perhaps because he found them too traditional and "conventional."[24] Any attempts to reformulate a garden's planting still tended to founder on the divergent and ambivalent directions of materials and their representation when compared to the materials of architecture.

When the architect Serge Chermayeff, who designed the wonderful modern De La Ware Pavilion at Bexhill-on-Sea in Sussex, came to build his own, again strikingly modern house at Bentley Wood, near Halland, he got Tunnard to design the garden. This featured an austere southern patio, with an eastern wall of slightly sculptured thin concrete and buttresses to hold it up, a simple pool against the wall, a statue by Henry Moore on a plinth, and a view beyond into a much cleared woodland with open grassland. It was photographed with modern deckchairs, not the usual *transatlantiques*.[25] These gestures, with Moore's *Recumbent Figure*, Nash's "dream" through the viewing frame, the concrete materials, unusual chairs, and a patio where a path stretches toward the view through the screen, all allow a convincingly modern garden to cohabit with the box-like building behind.

He worked on other gardens and projects, some of which were illustrated for him by Gordon Cullen (pp. 72–76). Nicely idiosyncratic, these include a weekend house at Cobham, Surrey, with swimming pool and architectural planting, and Tunnard's own place at St Ann's Hill (somewhat similar to the patio at Bentley Wood and featuring the sculpture by Willi Soukop), with a distant view of Halland (all these designs featured lawns). And they all suggest either a very minimalist landscape—with pavers set in the grass at Cobham and St Ann's Hill—or cubist flower beds and vegetable gardens, and all but one show people using them; the landscapes are represented to suggest the relationship of the modern building to Tunnard's landscape designs. These images of private gardens have an uncanny resemblance to some of the drawings that Lawrence Halprin would make for his private clients, mainly in California during the 1940s and 1950s.[26]

For the house Land's End, in Gaulby, Leicester (designed by Raymond McGrath), Tunnard, as well as Frank Clark, drew and redrew plans during the late 1930s, though the final authorship of the landscape is either debated or (inevitably) the result of the melding of various contributions. What seem to be in Tunnard's hand is again the open and irregular lawn surrounded by a series of gardens, some of which were set in rectangles in the manner of Guevrekian's Villa Noialles; perimeter walks that edged the site (in both format and the use of color to lengthen perspectives, those walks were a distinct eighteenth-century reference); a shelter or pavilion in the Japanese style overlooking a pond; and the sight of adjacent pinewoods drawn into the more manicured garden.

Where Tunnard's interests really seemed to develop, in the years immediately before he left for the United States in 1938, was in thinking about how to save and develop the eighteenth-century estate of Claremont and in the ideas that he devised for minimal housing plots. The Claremont proposals are set out in his text (pp. 149ff), but the housing projects are not. The latter were featured both in *Architecture Review* 85 (1939), which suggested ways to design a "standard" and suburban garden plot,[27] and in the exhibition devised with Clark for the Institute of Landscape Architects, as reported in an autumn issue of *Landscape and Garden* (1938). Tunnard's proposal for small suburban plots and how the garden elements might be varied or developed were a less intricate version of the same ideas that Garrett Eckbo was producing at Harvard's GSD in 1937 and 1938.[28] When he added plans and photographs of "Modern American Gardens" in the 1948 edition (pp. 167–74)—noting that it was "too soon to discern any distinct stylistic innovations"—he had clearly extended his English work through contacts with Eckbo and American practice.

In America he continued to design, providing gardens for two houses designed by Holmes Perkins. He worked on gardens around Cambridge for Carl Koch, a Harvard architecture alumnus, and also for a private garden in Rhode Island and gardens for the premises and museum of the New London Country Historical Society in Connecticut. He proposed designs for the sculpture garden at the Musuem of Modern Art (this was not implemented), but along with three young architects, won third prize in the competition for the Jefferson National Expansion Memorial (won by Eero Saarinen).[29] He also collaborated on the journal *Task*, issued by the GSD at Harvard, for which he wrote articles on regional planning in 1941, on the reprecussions of the war on "British" planning in the third issue, on Robert Moses and Portland, Oregon (issue 5), and, by then at Yale in 1948, on "Is architecture an art?"[30]

The afterlife of *Gardens in the Modern Landscape* concerns not only its historical origins—how it featured and functioned within the modernism of the 1930s—but also how we today still might find it useful. Originally, it had mixed reviews. Some were skeptical about its "modern" emphasis and felt that it would soon become a "period piece," while others found it thoughtful and provocative.[31] The rich, but also eclectic, ideas that Tunnard espoused and wrestled with may yield an agenda of topics today, especially when landscape architecture seems to be trying, not always successfully, to invent a new image and function for itself that "landscape urbanism" or "ecological urbanism" has sought. Back in 1958, twenty years after the 1938 edition, Ian Mcharg wrote to Tunnard asking for suggestions as to what book he would recommend to be "most indicative of the path towards the design of open space to 20th century society";[32] there was nothing, then or now, that leapt to mind.

The historical importance of *Gardens in the Modern Landscape* is that it was one of the few books to confront the role of garden making in international modernism. Tunnard was far ahead of his time (and may still be, though only by being paradoxically *retarditaire*). That his book did not fully succeed in making or establishing that role was the result partly of the confusion and complexity of ideas with which Tunnard was wrestling and partly because landscape architecture has never found that task easy; it continues to argue its way awkwardly into the mainstreams of modern thinking, not least because it is self-confessedly atavistic, especially in garden designs, which continue to flourish even when landscape architects value ambitious endeavors in the public sphere over the making of private gardens that tend to be more traditional. The garden exhibition he designed with Frank Clark in 1939 was, as he explained in a catalog entry, about how "in one way or another landscape architects play a part in every form of out-of-door planning and fulfill a function that is as vital to the community as that of their collaborators, the architect and the engineer."[33] He rooted for modernism (perhaps not realizing that there were multiple modernisms) and then renounced it; but modernism as he found it in architecture was not easily or necessarily apt for landscape architecture, yet his eye for good work such as Amsterdam's Bos Park still locates him firmly in the vanguard. The original dust jacket of the 1938 edition makes this emblematically clear: one of Gordon Cullen's drawings of a

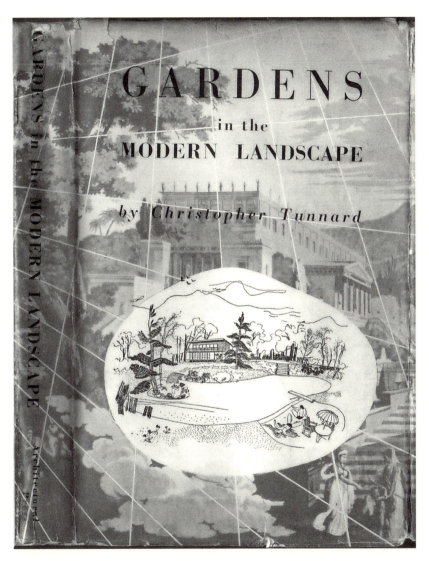

The original dust jacket of the 1938 edition. *Courtesy of Jan Woudstra.*

modern garden floats uneasily against a background that features a classical structure of a Claudean landscape painting.

However, Tunnard's book also makes clear what must still be deemed central to the field. It was often witty and ironic (see pp. 14 or 49, for instance), and this sits uneasily with the solemn professionalism today. And he used his rhetorical skills to plead for the expansion of the garden into a larger landscape that these days includes not only the items that Tunnard identified—housing estates, factories, urban parkland, recreational sites—but also derelict factories and steel mills and unwanted industrial riverscapes. And that means we should welcome his insistence on cross-disciplinary collaboration between design and planning (essentially recapitulating his own career). He valued also preservation, and came to do so even more after this book was published, and preservation stimulates creative rethinking ("creative urbanism" as it has been called[34]). Then there is the need to marry function with beauty, for despite his nervousness about that b-word, no landscape architect that I know wants to design ugly places, and there are fresh ways of registering beauty in austere and empathic minimalism—beauty is still the elephant in the room for many landscape architects (and it rarely, if at all, occurs as part of their professional training). In addition, Tunnard was always committed to history, not as an anthology of styles and mechanical forms to be copied, but as an arsenal of ideas. He may have traveled with the "difficult baggage of history and horticulture,"[35] but landscape architects still need to know their plants, while an emphasis on landscape and urban history as a resource and stimulus stops designers from reinventing the wheel without knowing it.[36]

Notes

1. A portion of a paragraph on "beauty" in 1938 (p. 94) was discarded on p. 93 of 1948. See n. 11 below.

2. Tunnard himself wrote "Modern Gardens for Modern Houses: Reflections on Current Trends in Landscape Design" in the *Bulletin* of the Garden Club in September 1941, where he saw gardens as "stages," with "every occupant a player."

3. Here p. 61. He was still going on about Sharawadgi in his last book, *A World with a View: An Inquiry into the Nature of Scenic Values* (New Haven, Conn.: Yale University Press, 1978), 76–87.

4. The rearrangement of image clusters is: the 1938 frontispiece moves to p. 68 in 1948; the section on Pain's Hill gets moved from pp. 25–32 to pp. 27–34 here; plans on different layouts at different periods (1938, pp. 129–32) get moved to pp. 134–37.

5. Thus p. 26 uses an image from "The Garden House" section (1938, p. 170); another garden house from 1938, p. 171, moves to p. 42; a sculpture by Willi Soukop is moved from 1938, p. 180, to p. 98 , and a conservatory from 1938 p. 182 to p. 117 here.

6. I am indebted to Lance Neckar, who has published two essays on Tunnard: "Strident Modernism/Ambivalent Reconsiderations," *Journal of Garden History* 10 (1990): 237–46,

and "Christopher Tunnard: The Garden in the Modern Landscape," in *Modern Landscape Architecture: A Critical Review,* ed. Marc Treib (Cambridge, Mass.: MIT Press, 1993), 144–58. Also the more recent study by David Jacques and Jan Woudstra, *Landscape Modernism Renounced: The Career of Christopher Tunnard (1910–1979)* (New York: Routledge, 2009). This last announces on its title page "contributions by Elen Deming, David Jacques, Lance Neckar, Ann Satterthwaite and Jan Woudstra," but the text itself does not identify them individually. It amasses a wealth of new information, somewhat unevenly packaged and not always easy to use.

7. He tried to make sense of his career in a late book, *A World with a View.* His early curiosity was fueled by the endless books he seems to have borrowed from the Lindley Library of the Royal Horticultural Society, details of which loans are cited by Jacques and Woudstra (see their index).

8. "Tunnard: The Modernist with a Memory," *Landscape Design* (October 1987): 20–23.

9. *The Art and Architecture of English Gardens* (New York: Rizzoli, 1989), chap. 5, "The Modern Movement Garden," 179–85.

10. 1948, p. 6. This is not listed in Jacques and Woudstra's checklist of writings, though its text is reproduced on pp. 91–92. But it is extensively commented upon in Dorothée Imbert, *Between Garden and City: Jean Canneel-Claes and Landscape Modernism* (Pittsburgh: University of Pittsburgh Press, 2009), 113–17; she notes that Canneel-Claes's name alone appears on the pamphlet, but that the English version "acknowledge[s] the influence of Tunnard."

11. This deleted section reads: "After discussing the uses of gardens, it is customary to talk about their beauties. We are relieved from the monotony of investigating this relative factor if we accept the fact that beauty is but a by-product of the creative attitude to garden planning. We do not aim at the creation of beauty, although it accepts this quality as a logical accompaniment of the artistic fact. One does not bake bread primarily for the sake of enjoying its flavor, but for nourishment, and the degree of nourishment provided by any work of art is now generally recognized as the only test of its value" (1938, p. 94). He continued his concern with aesthetics in a paper ("The Art of Landscape Architecture") read at an Ann Arbor Conference on Aesthetic Evaluation, a typescript of which is held in the Architectural Archives of the University of Pennsylvania.

12. 1938, p. 98, and with a brief discussion of it on p. 101; p. 93 here.

13. That he "clearly had a mind for theorising" seems dubious, at least for his landscape writings: Jacques and Woudstra, 85.

14. Ibid., 16 and 18.

15. Ibid., 101, which discusses these contacts.

16. Tunnard wrote "Landscape Design at the Paris International Congress: What Other Countries Are Doing," *Landscape & Garden* (Summer 1937): 78–82.

17. Jacques and Woudstra, 28. Hermelin is quoted at length in 1938 (pp. 77–78) and in 1948 (p. 76).

18. Jacques and Woudstra, 115. But architectural plants had been a feature that William Robinson, whom Tunnard credits with rudely awakening Victorian gardeners (pp. 55–59), admired in Parisian parks; see William Robinson, *Parks, Promenades, and Gardens of Paris* (1869), plate XV and the same kind of architectural plant examples illustrated in Jean-Charles-Adolphe Alphand, *Les Promenades de Paris* (1867–73).

19. A garden by Powell, illustrated in 1938 and 1948 (p. 71), this repeats the well-known design of Guevrekian's garden at Hyères in France (facing it on p. 70); Hill designed a garden for the British Pavilion at the 1937 Paris show.

20. Cited Jacques and Woudstra, 33.

21. The first two paintings are illustrated in Margot Eates, *Paul Nash: The Master of the Image 1889–1946* (London: John Murray, 1973), figs. 89 and 53b, respectively.

22. I am grateful here for the discussion of this topic by David Leatherbarrow, *The*

Roots of Architectcural Invention: Site, Enclosure, Materials (Cambridge: Cambridge University Press, 1993), 1–6, from which I quote in my text, with my italics.

23. If these are indeed Holmes's annotations (it is certainly his copy), p. 133, in the Rare Book Room of the Fine Arts Library, University of Pennsylvania. He also writes "simplicity" in the margin (1938, p. 67) when Tunnard calls for "a new simplicity in gardens" (p. 67); otherwise, the only annotations are pencil marks alongside various paragraphs.

24. Quoted in Jacques and Woudstra, 115.

25. See image in 1948, p. 68. Other images of the wall are in Brown, figs. 23 and (for the wall) 24. Tunnard's various garden projects, which cannot be discussed fully in this context, are discussed fully in Jacques and Woudstra, though the relevant discussions are somewhat scattered through the volume. This is especially useful for Tunnard's work at Gaulby, see below.

26. See Alison Hirsch, "Lawrence Halprin: The Choreography of Private Gardens," *Studies in the History of Gardens and Designed Landscapes* 27, no. 4 (2007), being a collection of and commentary on Halprin's drawings and plans of American gardens in the Architectural Archives of the University of Pennsylvania. Halprin records both his discovery of Tunnard's book in Wisconsin ("I realized it was speaking my language") and his subsequent work under him at Harvard in *A Life Spent Changing Places* (Philadelphia: University of Pennsylvania Press, 2011); Halprin also records Tunnard's "helping" Philip Johnson with his garden, pp. 42–45.

27. These suburban garden ideas are illustrated in Jacques and Woudstra, 37, 39, and 40.

28. See Marc Treib and Dorothée Imbert, *Garret Eckbo: Modern Landscape for Living* (Berkeley: University of California Press, 1997), 33–38. When Eckbo, Dan Kiley, and James Rose wrote their articles on primeval, rural, and urban environments in *Architectural Record* (1939–40), Tunnard was referred to as "the English landscapist."

29. Some of these American designs are discussed and illustrated in Jacques and Woudstra, 165–78.

30. These issues have been scanned at Harvard: http://pds.lib.harvard.edu/pds/view/45295213.

31. Jacques and Woudstra, 1 and 35–36.

32. Ibid., 235–36, citing the Tunnard Yale archives.

33. From catalog entry for the exhibition "Garden and Landscape," organized by the Institute of Landscape Architecture and held at the Royal Institute of British Architects. See Jacques and Woudstra, 38ff.

34. Jacques and Woudstra, 218.

35. Neckar, "The Garden in the Modern Landscape," 144.

36. The first half of Tunnard's book *The City of Man* (New York: Scribner's, 1953) was firmly grounded in history, and he acknowledged a special debt to Henry Hope Reed, a determined nay-sayer on modernism.

GARDENS
IN THE MODERN LANDSCAPE

First edition printed 1938
Second (revised) edition printed 1948

Printed in Great Britain by
Billing and Sons Ltd., Guildford and Esher
Press

GARDENS
IN THE MODERN LANDSCAPE

By Christopher Tunnard

Associate Professor of City Planning, Yale University

**Second (revised) edition with new material on
American Gardens, and a note on the Modern
Garden by Dean Joseph Hudnut of Harvard University**

London: The Architectural Press
New York: Charles Scribner's Sons

CONTENTS

FOREWORD

IT is now ten years since the material in these pages first appeared in *The Architectural Review*. Very little creative work has been done during the interval owing to the war. The author, like everyone else, has been engaged in other occupations, with little time for reflection on the charm of natural things; but since it is his publisher's and his own opinion that the book should reappear very much in its original form, a few remarks on conclusions reached during this relatively inactive period may not come amiss.

The opinion expressed in the book that the eighteenth-century invention of landscape gardening was among the most notable of British contributions to the arts has been reinforced by observation in America, where, as an article for export, it seems to have again proved its excellence. Some day an account must be given of the English tradition in America and of the translation of the ideas of Langley, Repton, Price and Gilpin along the James River, up the Hudson and in New England. This must be done before the great estates of the Eastern seaboard go the way of their English counterparts, as they will do, in spite of the efforts of the National Park Service—the American equivalent of our National Trust—unless the public is sufficiently aroused.

The author's original rather cursory estimate of the nineteenth century has undergone considerable revision as the result of further investigations, which have proved that the inventions of our grandfathers and great-grandfathers often possessed great daring and originality. This opinion is based on the discovery that the nineteenth-century revivals were not always mere essays in copyism, but actually productive of entirely new forms and expressions. Our attitude of hasty condemnation may well give way to one of considerable respect as the full story unfolds. More power to those who have begun to encourage an interest in our immediate past!

The author's attitude toward modern art, architecture and landscape architecture has also changed somewhat as the result of seeing more examples. This has not been surprising to him, nor will it be to his readers, since the movement is avowedly experimental and no one remotely connected with it can be expected to stand pat on opinions formed at an earlier stage of development.

Most important perhaps is the conviction that creative art has a firmer foundation when based on the accumulation of acquired knowledge rather than on intuitiveness alone. In 1937, the author, together with the Belgian landscape architect, Jean Caneel-Claes, wrote a manifesto which contained among its clauses the following:

We believe in the probity of the creative act . . . the reliance of the designer on his own knowledge and experience and not on the academic symbolism of the styles or outworn systems of æsthetics, to create by experiment and invention new forms which are significant of the age from which they spring.

Time has proved, to at least one of its writers, that this statement should be modified. If one is attempting to grow a rare plant, the natural procedure is to look up the work of previous cultivators in order to avoid mistakes, and then perhaps to add a dash of initiative by varying the formula to suit the special conditions of the situation and climate. In artistic development, this method seems also to be useful. May one say with fairness that there are too many architects and others who adopt a " modern " style without regard to its origins or philosophy ? These are the people who are defeating true modernism; they do not investigate enough; they have discarded the older styles without bothering to find out what they represent or the demands of the society which produced them. It is not surprising that the more forward-looking practitioners regret this gap in their training, or that many have now begun to study the methods of past times in order to salvage what may be useful to them in cultivating their artistic growth. There is no reason in the world why this should hinder their use of new materials and techniques, as has often been supposed. The free, untrammelled creator may be an engaging personality, but he may also be out of touch with the needs of the times, and commit some frightful blunder when faced with a situation requiring exact economic, artistic, or historical knowledge.

A professor in an " advanced " college in North Carolina who read the first edition of this book recommended that the next one should contain less history and " more modern things." The author's reply was a quotation from Geoffrey Scott: " That which has once genuinely pleased is likely again to be found pleasing," and a rejoinder to the effect that, in England at any rate, by far the best work was done over a hundred years ago. The aphorism is all too true, and it is especially true of planning and architecture which are always better when they acknowledge precedent.

" If the modern movement does not achieve recognition in the next five years, it will be dead." The distinguished head of a modern school of architecture and planning said this recently in conversation with the author. People in his position have had ample opportunity to observe the results of the system; the first courses in modern architecture in America were given at the University of Michigan as long ago as the late twenties. The statement is a considerable challenge to those of us who in the twenties and thirties started out with high hopes and a good deal of faith in the new art forms, and it hovers like the hand of fate over the heads of those even younger people who have recently been trained in no other medium. It is a challenge, however, that can be met. It may be agreed that the modern movement has drifted into many curious forms and mannerisms. If the current mannerist style continues, its death will come from public indifference. "A style for our own times" may not be anything like what we imagined a few years ago: perhaps it should, in fact, be more like what was current a hundred years ago—a meshing of several styles or idioms with entirely dissimilar physical results. In other words, the modernist ought now to be broadening his range, not narrowing it, and trying his hand at all sorts of solutions. In his otherwise delightful book, *British Architects and Craftsmen*, Sacheverell Sitwell criticizes Wyatt for turning from Greek to Gothic and displaying what the present writer considers a pleasing versatility. To have several ways of building and planning at one's command ought to be the modern aim as well. "The pleasures of infinite variety" are sorely needed in the modern landscape, and the notions of Sharawadgi, which are mentioned in these pages, and have come much into prominence since the book was first published, might well have a present-day application. There should be no one style of building or planning.

A word should be added on the social aspects of modernism. There is a dangerous fallacy in thinking that a certain kind of architecture or planning is intrinsically "better" than another. From this stems the idea that its widespread use will help to build a better society. But architecture and physical planning have never shaped society; although planners have presumably been shaped by the society in which they live. The Bath and Regent Street that we admire were not the products of a particularly progressive society; and certainly they were not "good" for anyone, except a handful of middle class tradesmen, two or three architects and a couple of earls. On reflection, it will appear that the *programme* of physical planning is the agent which influences society and that which the programme produces will be determined by what it says and who writes it. Architects and allied technicians *must* go into community planning—they are badly needed—but while they may help shape the plan, they should not try to dictate its final form. We must beware of the approach of the technocrat, of anti-intellectual reliance on "intuition," of metaphysical formulæ and of the so-called biological or "organic" approach, which may be suitable when discussing the relative merits of fertilizers, but does not belong in the socio-economic process of town planning. When attempted there, as in Wright's Broadacre City, this approach results in something which could never be built and which no one would want to live in if it were.

So much for the philosophy of the subject. The author's personal approach to landscape gardening and planning has not changed. First, an eighteenth century understanding of " the genius of the place " is necessary. Then the structure—in which usefulness and æsthetic pleasure must both be considered. Then materials of only the best quality (when they are available!)—this is very important, and it will be noticed that they are put in their proper place, after the grand conception, not before it. Finally, understanding the wishes of the client, whether it is a private citizen or a public committee in New York or London. This formula does not result in mannerism, to the best of the writer's knowledge and experience.

With this opportunity to put the last word first, the reader may be left to the book itself. Except for a slight condensation and a few corrections, the text is unchanged. At the suggestion of several readers of *The Architectural Review*, some sketches of plants which appeared in that periodical have been included in this edition. The postscript, which originally appeared in the *Bulletin* of the Garden Club of America, is by Joseph Hudnut, who may perhaps best be described to English readers as Sir Charles Reilly's counterpart in the United States. Architects and designers in America have gained much from his generous support; not least among them the author, who owes him his introduction to a new field of activity.

CHRISTOPHER TUNNARD.

Yale University, 1948.

A C K N O W L E D G E M E N T S

The author's thanks are due to H. F. Clark for help in the preparation of the text and illustrations, to T. Gordon Cullen, Lloyd Flood and L. B. Voiṭ for sketches, to Arthur Sanderson and Sons, Ltd., for permission to reproduce, as the background to the bookjacket, a portion of their photograph of a wall-paper from the panoramic sequence entitled " Telemachus on the Island of Calypso" printed by Dufour about 1825, to the Studio for the loan of the block on page 92, to Letitia Hicks-Beach for the drawings of St. Ann's Hill, to Hugh Macdonald for Shenstoniana, to Bernard Leach for information concerning Japanese art, to A. G. Ling and John Piper for photographs, to Raymond McGrath for illustrations from his book " Twentieth Century Houses," to the Royal Institute of British Architects for permission to use its blocks of the Amsterdam Boschplan, to the Keeper of the Royal Horticultural Society's Library, F. J. Chittenden, for permission to photograph illustrations in old horticultural works, and to W. T. Stearn of the same institution for assistance with references and the bibliography. The author also desires to thank Mrs. Combe and L. A. D'A. D'Engelbronner for permission to photograph the gardens at Pain's Hill and Redleaf, and Herbert Felton for the execution of this work. Finally, he records his appreciation of the advice and criticism given him by H. de C. Hastings and J. M. Richards of The Architectural Review, in which magazine a large portion of the book was originally published in serial form, and by M. A. Regan and A. E. Doyle (the latter particularly for the format and lay-out) of The Architectural Press.

8

LANDSCAPE INTO GARDEN

I—Reason and Romanticism

A GARDEN is a work of art. It is also a number of other things, such as a place for rest and recreation, and for the pursuit of horticulture, but to be a garden in the true sense of the term it must first be an æsthetic composition.

The necessity for keeping this in mind arises from a two-centuries old confusion between the idea of gardens as pure works of art, and as works of art in imitation of nature. When Addison said, " Gardens are works of art, therefore they rise in value according to the degree of their resemblance to nature," he propounded the most fallacious argument that it has ever been the lot of the landscape artist to try to confute. It was perhaps inevitable that, already using her own materials, the pursuers of this art who had just begun to break free from deep-rooted fears of nature as a tyrannical mother, and who now began to woo her as a mistress, should on occasions have confused the means with the end; even so, it could hardly be expected that Addison's initial error should have led others down the strange and tortuous paths which have brought the modern landscape architect to his present anomalous position. Painters, poets, novelists, musicians and architects were all dragged through the mire, so it is hardly surprising that the fashionable eighteenth-century landscape gardeners did not emerge with their artistic integrities unstained; the matter for regret is that their counterparts of today have not profited by the experience of brother artists who, in almost every sphere of æsthetic

9

activity, have wiped the mud from their shoes and set off on a straighter road towards a more clearly defined horizon.

The occasion of Addison's visit to Italy, which roughly corresponds with the opening of the eighteenth century, marked the end of one literary age and the beginning of another. It also sounded the death knell of the old " formal " style of gardening. The next forty years saw the most complete revolution in gardening taste which the art has ever known; our quarrel, however, is not with the influence of that period, but of a later one. The earlier landscape gardeners contributed much to the enlargement of artistic experience—they gave us incidentally the familiar outlines of our present countryside —and although their work contained the germ which gave rise to the subsequent æsthetic malady of gardens, these painters in nature's materials, as they have been called, were only its harmless carriers.

For an exact diagnosis it will be necessary to examine the development of gardens together with the artistic trends of the last two hundred years. At the beginning of this period, particularly, gardening was influenced by painting and literature in a manner so marked that these two arts have from the first been recognized as affecting English landscape design more strongly than the economic upheaval which was just beginning.* " The Greeks had no Thomsons because they had no Claudes " was an often quoted saying of the latter part of the century, and while English poets formed their taste on a study of Italian paintings, landscape gardeners drew their inspiration from both. A small acquaintance with the literary and artistic thought of the period makes it clear that gardening followed literature and painting fairly closely, and not architecture, as some writers would have us believe. On the contrary, this latter art was influenced by gardens to a certain extent. Certainly the revived cult of the Gothic in architecture first appeared in gardens, into which ruined abbeys and crumbling castles were introduced as likely to induce the feeling of pensive melancholy, considered a highly satisfactory reaction in the spectator of a landscape garden.

This inter-reaction of the governing ideals of painting, literature and gardening began with the enthusiasm for Italian landscape as seen through the eyes of painters like Claude and Salvator, and as elaborated in the writings of travellers who had made the Grand

---

* Inclosure was largely the means of humanizing the landscape. The Inclosure Commissioners divided hundreds of parishes into neat square fields, the regularity of which to a great extent must have helped to create the contemporary feeling that " all Nature was a garden."

Tour, such as Addison, Thomson, Dyer, Gray, and, later, Horace Walpole. The serene and glowing landscapes of Claude and the romantic savagery of Salvator were thought typical in the first case of the Italian plains and the country round Rome and in the second of the wilderness of the Alps through which the English usually passed, at some hazard to their personal safety, on the journey to Italy. Paintings of both these artists found their way across the water and were praised above those of the Dutch masters in which the classical touch so much admired by the new generation of history-conscious " men of taste " was disappointingly absent. The Italian style was feverishly copied and England became a nation of amateur artists.

Was it not perhaps natural that those who found themselves only mediocre painters in oils and still wished to be accounted as following the fashion should turn to the new style of gardening when it evolved, as a supposedly more facile means of expression? Landscape gardening became the hobby of every English gentleman, and a resulting confusion of ideals was thus perhaps only to be expected.

The point to make clear is that the seventeenth-century formal style, degenerate and cluttered with absurdities of decoration as it became, was an art in a sense that the landscape style was not. Though bound by innumerable sets of rules, an artist like Le Nôtre was at liberty to indulge his creative instincts without the

Top, a pre-landscape garden. Bottom, " . . . the apparatus of a rude and hearty taste in outdoor amusement." From " Systema Horticulturæ," J. Worlidge, London, 1677.

11

necessity of producing a representational design.   Within the limits of his walls and hedges there was room for free play of the imagination. The landscape gardeners set themselves no limit; the boundaries of their garden were the shores of England; but they were fettered by the conventional necessity for pictorial imitation.

What other features can be marked as revealing the essential nature of the landscape movement ?   To begin with, it did not arise simply " as a reaction to the excessively dull formal style of gardening," as the change is passed over by many of the gardening histories. Every reaction is caused by new ideas; without them each generation would remain content with the manners and makeshifts of its forefathers.   Art follows the inventions of science, the changing standards of economics, and the adventurous feet of pioneers of exploration, and the period under review was not lacking in all three.   We have begun to see how gardening was influenced in the highest degree by the arts of painting and literature.   The " pleasing, horrid and enchanted " Chinese garden of which Europe in the early eighteenth century had romantic but unauthenticated descriptions, remains the unknown quantity in this process of change.   But such major events as the passing of the Inclosure Acts, the economic upheaval loosely referred to as the Industrial Revolution, the exploration of China and Japan by Jesuit missionaries, and the new interest aroused in the history of the Middle Ages among a class which hitherto had only been appalled by its barbaric aspects, all played their parts in the determining of the new landscape.

This landscape, before being taken into the garden and developed outwards from the house windows, already existed in the imaginations of men of taste, and without its help our Kents and Browns could hardly have made the rapid strides they did in public favour. Brown's ridiculous clumps and mounds would have been laughed out of existence a good deal less laboriously than they were removed a generation later under the direction of Repton, had they not been softened by the background of trees which landowners had planted, frightened by the denudation of the countryside of timber used for shipbuilding and the development of towns during the reigns of the Tudors. Evelyn's *Sylva* had made a plea for the replacement of the national forests as early as 1664, and up to the end of the first third of the eighteenth century, when the wealthy classes had profited by his example and increased the stock, in almost every gardening and agricultural treatise one reads a plea for the replenishment of natural resources. " Improvement" was an accomplished practice in Restoration times before being recognized as a fashionable one in the age which followed.

12

" Perhaps the landskips of Poussin are the best instructor which a gardener of genius and taste can follow " (Essay on the Different Natural Situations of Gardens : Samuel Ward, 1774). Above is Nicholas Poussin's landscape, " Phocion," illustrating the qualities of " picturesque " composition which were to be translated into the eighteenth-century garden.

Other existing factors helped the bold Kent to " forge a great system from the twilight of imperfect essays." The stiff brick-walled gardens of William III and his gardening queen had been relaxed at their margins by the introduction of grilles and iron railings, imported, together with the taste for pug dogs and pineapples, from the " Dutch morass," and these former, with the help of the new gates of wrought iron, also introduced by William, enabled the eye to glance through to the plantations beyond. What more inevitable than the transition from the half-wall to the railing and thence to the ha-ha, a sinking of the ground in the form of a ditch, at this time to be seen in France where it formed part of a system of military defence ? And once the wall was down, there was no ignoring the landscape; something had to be done about untidy woods and fields that could be seen from the parterre. Kent's famous leap, therefore, had it not been merely a figure of speech, would in any case have called for small athletic prowess.

13

The hint of French influence in an art considered so unreservedly British in origin, has not so far proved very disturbing to horticultural historians. But Johnson,* whose information is usually reliable, mentions Dufresnoy, the successor of Le Nôtre, as being a creator of landscape parks in France in the year 1700, which is at least a decade before they were attempted in England. According to this author, " his example was only admired by his countrymen and not followed." Any of Dufresnoy's works might have been seen by Addison during his travels in France before the historic essays were written. One would hardly like to accuse the French public of having seen the landscape garden, dismissing it as altogether ridiculous and illogical, and sending the device that made it possible over the Channel to confound the English, who might be depended upon to play the idea to death while its Machiavellian originators in the wings laughed up their elegant, silken sleeves. It is, however, significant that later, when the French introduced Chinoiserie to Europe, they were inclined to restrict the innovations to garden architecture, tea pavilions, porcelain guinguettes and the like, and to disregard in great measure the Oriental abhorrence of avenue planting in straight lines. It is fairly safe to say that the majority of the French people remained faithful to the straight line even at the end of the eighteenth century when the cult of " zigzag shrubberies and wheelbarrow mounts " was at its height in Europe.

Not so the English. " Is there anything more shocking than a stiff, regular garden? " asks Batty Langley in 1728, and proceeds to add weight to the claim by diversifying his own creations with winding valleys, dales, purling streams, serpentine meanders, enclosures of corn, wood-piles, precipices, cold baths and cabinets, to name but a few of the fifty odd component parts of " a beautiful rural garden." Regularity is a term which could scarcely be applied to scenes which included all the appurtenances of the old gardens, together with some of the new, and with the paraphernalia of rusticity thrown in. In this last he was anticipating the Wordsworthian ideals of rural beauty, but it was an early stage at which to confuse still further the imitators of Claude and Salvator, in whose paintings this quality had not so far been applauded. Doubtless their followers were quick to see in Lorraine's *The Ford* and similar works the symbol which they must at once have hurried to find.

The gardens of Langley, Switzer, Addison, Pope† and Bridgeman,

---

* *A History of English Gardening*, George W. Johnson, London, 1829.

† Pope's observations on gardening reveal an interest in the mechanics rather than the æsthetics and little appreciative grasp of the growing landscape style. Spence gives an account of his idea for planting " an old Gothic cathedral in trees " in which " good large poplars with their white stems (cleared of boughs to a proper

14

if it had not been for their medley of styles (Addison saw no reason why the Chinese and Queen Anne gardens should not be amalgamated in harmony), were by reason of their transitional nature more closely related to our present-day compromise of formality and informality than anything in the two hundred years between. The decorative scroll work of the parterre garden had been done away with during the reign of Anne, who had the parterre at Windsor covered with turf. Thus the ground near the house remained geometrical, but plain, and must have approximated to the modern terrace. Beyond lay " formal " gardens, usually with basins of water and fountains prominently displayed, and beyond that again the wilderness, albeit a wilderness more productive and entertaining than Elijah's. Menageries, mirrors, waterworks, cones of fruit trees, and bird cages, were all relics of the age of William and Mary and of Louis XIV: the apparatus of a rude and hearty taste in outdoor amusement, soon to be superseded by the affectations of sentiment. The plan of Pope's garden made by his gardener Serle in 1744 is typical of the more restrained lay-outs of this time.

But whereas the tendency of the future will probably be away from " natural " gardening towards an architectural style, that is, away from unplanning towards conscious and balanced arrangement, the swing in those days was in the other direction. It is well known that during the dictatorships of Brown, Wright, Holland and Eames, flowers and flower-beds were practically abolished from English gardens. Such frippery would have disgraced " by discordant character the contiguous lawn." Yet the earlier landscapists had no

---

height) would serve very well for the columns; and might form the different aisles or peristilliums, by their different distances and heights." As with the majority of his contemporaries, the towering beauty of the poplar could not be appreciated for its own sake; it had to be made either part of a picture or given some antique or sentimental value which appealed to the imagination. "The management of surprises " involved an appreciation of this point of view. Pope summed up his attitude to gardening in the following couplet:

> " He gains all ends, who pleasingly confounds,
> Surprises, varies, and conceals the bounds."

This might, in fact, have been an epitome of his methods of writing verse. The scrupulous search for perfection pursued by the classicists and exhibited in the balanced orderliness of such masterpieces of the prosodic style as *The Rape of the Lock* or *Windsor Forest* would in any case have made Pope unfitted for the pursuit of wild nature. It is true that *Windsor Forest* bears traces of the earlier lyricism which characterized the Pastorals, but this is rarely to be found in his later works. A younger Pope might have been truly the first landscape gardener; as it was, his interest in the art was aroused too late.

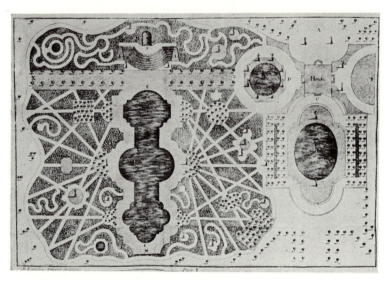

The beginnings of irregularity : from " New Principles of Gardening," Batty Langley, London, 1728.

such ruthless ideas. They had as yet few theories about colour, although they had been forced to cultivate a rather unwilling taste for the sombre reds and browns of autumn by academicians of the day, and were particular about the distribution of light and shade, which Kent effected by means of evergreen and variegated shrubs. Flowers were still to them the " wholesome herbs " of Shakespeare, in spite of the findings of expeditions to America and China; ignorance of the cultural requirements of new species at this time led too often to failure and distrust of any but the better-known favourites, " the jessamine, violet, lily, gilly flower and carmine rose."

The flowers with which Shenstone adorned his ornamental farm were of this kind. One can regard Shenstone, poet, essayist, and man of taste, as a typical artist of the first phase of the landscape movement. He was, of course, an amateur, but then some of the most admired of landscape gardens, Hagley, Persfield, Stourhead and Pain's Hill, were laid out or developed by amateurs, with the great Price and Knight leading the host of gentlemen turned gardeners. He lacked pretension to architectural knowledge, in an age when every man was his own architect; he could never have achieved Kent's perfect little temples at Stowe, for instance; but without this, his poetic and pictorial gift sufficed in abundance for the charm of " The Leasowes," which he laid out to the admiration and envy of his many friends.

16

Apart from the regrettable occupation of the place by fairies, whose presence, together with his reputation for indolence, have always detracted from a general appreciation of their author's serious intentions towards art, the pictorial arrangement of the woods and fields, the grouping of ornament, and the management of water (of which we have exact descriptions), represent the culmination of all the confused gropings of that time towards a consistent technique. Shenstone had imagination and created pictures; the garden is a series of them, compositions in melancholy, pensiveness, and (we cannot judge, but are prepared to take another's word for it) " sublimity," the three tenets of his artistic faith, founded upon a study of Burke and the painters. " Pleasing the imagination by scenes of grandeur, beauty and variety," was the sum of his demands of the garden as a whole.

For the reason already given and because of a lack of money, Shenstone left " The Leasowes " remarkably unadorned with buildings. On his arrival " he cut a straight walk through his wood, terminated by a small building of rough stone; and in a sort of gravel or marlepit, in the corner of a field, amongst some hazels, he had scooped out a sort of cave, stuck a little cross of wood over the door, and called it an hermitage; and, a few years after, had built an elegant little summer-house in the water, under a fine group of beeches " (which was afterwards removed by Mr. Pitt's advice). He had not, Graves goes on to say, " then conceived the place as a whole "; when he did he was far-seeing enough not to crowd the scene with bricks and mortar or to dot the open space with clumps of trees,* but

> " taught the level plain to swell
> In verdant mounds, from whence the eye
> Might all their larger works descry,"

and was careful to frame his vistas on the neighbouring landscape, instead of some object near at hand, as Kent and Hamilton were content to do. Though reputedly always in debt, he managed to embellish his grounds on a mere £300 a year, while Hamilton at Pain's Hill, an estate modelled from the pictures of Poussin and the Italian masters, is reputed (no doubt with exaggeration) to have spent forty thousand pounds on the grotto alone.

In *Unconnected Thoughts on Gardening*, which has been already quoted, the technique of the artist is revealed. Almost alone among his contemporaries, Shenstone grasps the principles of form in their

---

* ". . . To parcel out a lawn into knots of shrubbery, or invest a mountain in a garb of roses . . . would be like dressing a giant in a sarsenet gown, or a Saracen's head in a Brussels night-cap."—*Unconnected Thoughts on Gardening*.

B

widest implications, and suggests the modern method of planning in a single sentence. " In designing a house and gardens, it is happy when there is an opportunity of maintaining a subordination of parts; the house so luckily placed as to exhibit a view of the whole design." Price, hailed as the originator of our present-day gardens, said very much the same thing. But Shenstone's chief claim to fame among his contemporaries and the generations immediately following lies in the remark, " I think the landscape painter is the gardener's best designer," which was later widely quoted from *Unconnected Thoughts* as being in direct opposition to Addison's pronouncement on natural beauty. This remark has been attributed without very good foundation to Kent, but Graves says that, although Kent must have been aware of its implications, Shenstone was the first to make it public. He died in 1763 unconscious of posthumous fame in gardening and in literature, where he is now chiefly remembered as a precursor of the Romantic Movement. His " native elegance of mind " has always had an appeal for the French and his taste for elegiac fragments on urns and seats was not long in finding itself echoed in their gardens. Ermenonville was known as " The Leasowes of France " and contained an inscription to the poet's memory.

A view of Shenstone's garden at The Leasowes. " One can regard Shenstone, poet, essayist, and man of taste, as a typical artist of the first phase of the landscape movement."

THE GROTTO

A MANIFESTATION OF THE TASTE FOR "AWFUL BEAUTY" IN THE EIGHTEENTH-CENTURY GARDEN

VAUX-LE-VICOMTE

From France, where as a frame for sculpture or a shady retreat the grotto exists to grace the formal style, it was imported into England and became the toy of Evelyn and his contemporaries: later the rocky cave beloved of Salvator . . .

CLAREMONT

. . . finding its home at last as a means of escape to Arcadia in the gardens of the pictorial landscape style.

PAIN'S HILL

Here in the horrid gloom society shuddered with the poets. An elevating pastime? Yes, for beauty+horror=sublimity.

OATLANDS PARK

For upwards of 100 years the grotto was part of the background of English social life. This one contained a bath, made for the. Duke of Newcastle late in the 18th century. Each of the four chambers had a dominating shell motif, each passage its shaft of filtered daylight. Convex mirrors, the skeleton ribs of epiphytic fern, bright mineral ores and fragments of Italian sculpture were composed to form a design of such complexity that it occupied a man and his two sons for five years in its construction. The grotto was recently destroyed.

SAINT ANN'S HILL

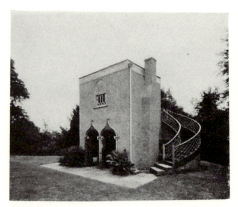

As a final example, a garden house with stalactite ceiling decorations, symbolical of that translation of garden romanticism into the sphere of architecture which was to affect so disastrously the architecture of the nineteenth century.

II— *The Verdant Age*

We enter upon the second half of the century with an awareness of the passing of rationalism—" the pleasure of being able to understand, the easy sense of simple orderliness, a smooth balance in ideas as in forms "—and the advent of a quickening sentimental feeling for the past, for exoticism and for the macabre. Poets now hymn their lays " by Tigris' Wandr'ing Waves," and the indigenous shepherdess of Shenstone's inspiration becomes the Persian Maid of Collins. Nature is worshipped more fervently than ever before, but she is beginning to be considered apart from her discoverers, the Salvators and Thomsons. The latter in the concluding parts of *The Seasons* even finds in her aspects other than those of serenity, savagery and universal omnipotence, while the disillusioned author of *Verses Written in London on the Approach of Spring* makes bold to question the capacity of the unchallenged masters:

> " Can rich Loraine mix up the glowing paint
> Bright as Aurora ? . . . Can savage Rosa
> With aught so wildly noble fill the mind,
> As where the ancient oak in the wood's depth
> . . . deserted stands ?"

The painter's conception of landscape having by this time become widely known, it was beginning to be recognized by a few as slightly artificial, selected, and untrue; in fact, though it was undoubtedly good art, there was just a possibility that it might be bad nature. The artistic pedestal was being removed and the goddess set upon her own feet.

Here is the root of a growing trouble.

We hurry through the intervening years, dodging the shaven hillocks and close-planted clumps of Brown, and passing with difficulty along the zigzag paths of Chambers' Eastern shrubberies, with nothing more interesting to stay us in our flight than a profusion of temples in conglomerate styles. Gothic and Oriental race neck and neck for supremacy, with Classic, a pale shadow, struggling behind. But when gardens belong to nature and no longer to painted nature, these edifices cease to serve their purpose, existing only to mock the new and echo a vanishing style. Symbolism is dying, and devotees of the new cult seek to justify the use of grottoes, caves and ruins by concealing in them cattle sheds and herdsmen's hovels or by designing

Top, a " picturesque " cottage for a retainer at Oatlands Park. Left, Kent's park at Claremont, as improved by Brown. The present mansion is reputed to be the only one ever built by Brown, although he altered many ; here the architectural magnificence at which he aimed has somehow not materialized. In 1850 it was possible to write that " . . . its present royal possessor . . . greatly enlarged the estate by the purchase of adjoining lands. These purchases were made to frustrate the speculating intentions of certain persons who were contemplating the erection of buildings around Claremont ; by which its domestic privacy, and sweet retirement, would have been destroyed." The irony of these remarks today will be appreciated after a glance at the photographs on pages 151 to 154.

them (how, we are not told) " in a manner naturalized to the trees and woods."

This period is the age of Lancelot Brown, who held undisputed sway, except for the jealous bickerings of Chambers, from 1750 until his death in 1783. This man, who refused work in Ireland because he " had not yet finished England," was a tremendous influence and not altogether an unmixed blessing to the country he was so zealous in " improving." He could rise to magnificent heights, as at Blenheim, which has always been considered his masterpiece, but he could also stoop so low as to indulge in constant repetition and to alter ground unnecessarily for the sake of performing this fascinating work. To smooth a rocky crag into a bald hummock was his especial delight, and one can only surmise that having observed the magical transformations achieved by levelling and grading, and lacking any satisfactory theory to justify his prodigious activities, this aspect of his work became an obsession with him in the manner of the bottle with the toper. In other words, he was far from being an artist, and his clients suffered for it. We, to whom the work of all eighteenth- and nineteenth-century landscapists appears softened by the mossy layers of time, are thankful to Brown and his followers for their tree planting, though even today their remaining overcrowded plantations of ill-assorted specimens bear testimony to a lack of skill in grouping.

The demand for Brown's services was enormous, not because he did good work but because improvements were the fashion. His genial manner won him popularity, and the literary and grammatical allusions with which he invariably illustrated his ideas no doubt helped to produce, in a gullible public, the sense of a competence which he was in fact far from possessing.

The landscape influence was felt in every garden in the land, from the surroundings of the palace to the enclosure of the smallest Thames-side villa. The two-acre estate of Squire Mushroom, the imaginary butt of Francis Coventry's wit in 1753, perhaps gives no very distorted view of the extremes in which landscaping could be taken:

" At your first entrance, the eye is saluted with a yellow serpentine river, stagnating through a beautiful valley, which extends near twenty yards in length. Over the rim is thrown a bridge ' partly in the Chinese manner,' and a little ship, with sails spread and streamers flying, floats in the middle of it. When you have passed this bridge, you enter into a grove perplexed with errors and crooked walks; where, having trod the same ground over and over again, through a labyrinth of hornbeam hedges, you are led into an old hermitage built with roots of trees, which the squire is pleased to call St. Austin's

23

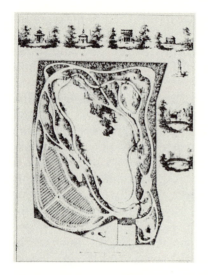

*The English garden in France . . . and the Chinese : from
" Plans Raisonnés de Toutes les Espèces de Jardins," Gabriel
Thouin, Cultivateur et Architecte de Jardins, Paris, 1820.*

cave. Here he desires you to repose yourself, and expects encomiums
on his taste: after which a second ramble begins through another maze
of walks, and the last error is much worse than the first. At length,
when you almost despair of ever seeing daylight any more, you emerge
on a sudden in an open and circular area, richly chequered with beds
of flowers, and embellished with a little fountain playing in the centre
of it. As every folly must have a name, the squire informs you, that
' by way of whim,' he has christened this place ' little Maribon,' at the
upper end of which you are conducted into a pompous, clumsy, and
gilded building, said to be a temple, and consecrated to Venus; for no
other reason which I could learn, but because the squire riots here
sometimes in vulgar love with a couple of orange-wenches, taken from
the purlieus of the play-house.''

In the above we can identify the lake as the work of Brown, the
hermitage as Shenstone's, the temple as deriving from Kent and the
flower garden and grove as relics of good Queen Anne. Coventry
concludes by describing a villa as " the chef-d'œuvre of modern
impertinence," an epithet which points to the fact that the planning
of villa gardens was looked upon as unimportant. The same attitude
is regrettably prevalent today.

Brown's death increased the numbers and fervour of the Brown-

24

ists, who before long completely outnumbered those who held that gardening should follow painting. These had a champion in Horace Walpole, who, as a connoisseur of the arts, commanded great respect, and in Whately, whose *Observations on Modern Gardening* was translated and had an influence on French taste. The Brownists, spurred on by the theory of an " S " " line of beauty " as promulgated by Hogarth, let this serpentine steed bear them as far as it would, falling back on the new warhorse of " utility " to carry them over the wider chasms in their argument. This latter term came into being when the inescapable difficulties in exploiting the picturesque point of view to its limit in gardens became apparent, though none could have been more impractical in his lay-outs than the master himself, who at Claremont carried the entrance to the servants' quarters underground so that the house could be entirely surrounded by lawn.

The phase we know as oriental gardening which enlivened proceedings at this stage was a by-product of the picturesque novel rather than an importation from China, and as developed by Chambers became an opportunity for indulging in ghoulish fancies like " The Valley of the Shadow of Death," which was incorporated in a pleasure garden (*sic*) near Dorking, and, decorated with coffins, skulls and appropriate inscriptions as to the vanity of man, gave a moral tone to the place which was thought highly edifying. In 1773 William Mason's *Heroic Epistle* so ridiculed this type of gardening that it quickly passed out of existence; the Chinese fashion in domestic and garden architecture, however, had as yet scarcely begun.

The followers of Brown and Nature gained ground; and unplanning arrived to stay. It is as well to remember that the essence of the better creations of the early landscapists lay in their appeal to the imagination and had certain features in common with the subtleties of the now well-known Japanese methods of evoking response to a work of art. When this appeal gave way to the lure of " natural " composition, unselected, disunited, and without a guiding principle, something was lost from English gardens: that something which made it impossible to recreate beauties such as those at Hagley or Persfield— monuments symbolic of an age and an ideal. The substitution of romance for sentiment ordered a change such as takes place in human relationships when passion succeeds friendship; but

A trio of Chambers' buildings at Kew, with ha-ha in right-hand foreground.

25

the passion of the romantic movement was unfulfilled; there was no consummation, only a vain striving after a perfection unobtainable within the limits of experience. And because this ideal was never realized, the movement degenerated into one of feeble and consolatory escapism. Irreconcilable Gothic castles and steam engines became its emblems and the puff-blown giants who had been its apostles sought refuge in moral theories or in idealistic philosophies.

An Early Gothic Revival garden house in stone, built about 1735-40 at Stourhead, Wilts, an estate which has recently come under the National Trust. There is only one room, which was originally furnished with farmhouse chairs and a table adorned with bones.

Above, a view to the house across the park. Below, a contemporary print of the lake, showing the grotto island.

A GARDEN
LANDSCAPE, 1740

Pain's Hill, Surrey

Top, *view from the house showing the evolution of eighteenth-century clump planting. Below, accompaniments to the pic-turesque scene . . ., left, the Roman mausoleum, and right, the ivy-clad Gothic ruin.*

Pain's Hill, one of the first and now the last of Surrey's celebrated landscape gardens, was being laid out in the 'forties and 'fifties of the eighteenth century by the Hon. Charles Hamilton, an amateur of the Picturesque. He planned the grounds " from the pictures of Poussin and the Italian masters," according to Mitford, among his other works being a waterfall at Bowood after a painting by Gaspar, and the grounds of his friend Charles James Fox. At the height of its fame the estate at Pain's Hill occupied about four hundred acres and was a centre of interest for the connoisseurs. Whately, Walpole and Uvedale Price were among the writers who praised its beauties, and even nineteenth-century historians, surrounded by the paraphernalia of a revived formalism in gardens, could find no fault:

" The demesne of Pain's Hill has long been celebrated as one of the earliest and finest examples of English landscape gardening. For this reputation it is indebted to Mr. Charles Hamilton, who was the first to take advantage of the natural disposition of the grounds, and with an artist's eye, and a refined judgment, strengthened by observation in foreign lands, so to distribute his plantations, and their artificial accompaniments,

28

Above, and inset, the Gothic temple, from which a series of "picturesque prospects" is obtained.

Right, the Watch Tower. Walpole compared the view from its summit to that of an Alpine forest. Below, a view of the serpentine lake.

Another view of the lake. On the left is the grotto island, and on the right, the " Alpine forest."

as both to create and command as rich a succession of picturesque and beautiful views as the situation could possibly afford."*

The " artificial accompaniments " to these picturesque scenes included a Gothic ruin, a grotto, a Roman mausoleum, a temple of Bacchus, a hermitage, a Turkish tent, and a Gothic temple of octagonal form. This last was restored in 1914, but the other buildings are in a state of dilapidation, with the exception of the hermitage, which was built of logs and gnarled roots and has long since disappeared. Hamilton is said to have hired an old man of venerable appearance to occupy this building, but the hermit soon grew tired of constant visitors and resigned.

Brayley goes on to say:

" On its north-east and south-east sides, Pain's Hill is bounded by the serpentine meanderings of the River Mole, which gives an irregular crescent-like form to that portion of the grounds. On the western side, the park is nearly level; but on the side next the river, the grounds are varied by boldly-swelling heights, interspersed with glades and valleys, more or less abrupt, and ranging in different directions."

It was these " boldly-swelling heights " that Walpole compared with an Alpine scene, " composed of pines, firs, a few birch, and such trees as assimilate with a savage and mountainous country." Of this part of Pain's Hill he says, " all is great and savage and rude; the walks seem not designed, but cut through the wood of pines; and

* *A Topographical History of Surrey*, Edward Wedlake Brayley, Volume 2, London, 1850.

Above, a lakeside view. The grass track borders the entire stretch of water. Left, Bramah's water wheel, thirty-two feet in diameter.

A tufa arch, through which the visitor passes on his way to the island grotto.

the style of the whole is so grand, and conducted with so serious an air of wild and cultivated extent, that when you look down on this seeming forest you are amazed to find it contain only a few acres."*

In Walpole's time, the Scots Pine was not the flourishing colonizer in Surrey that it has since become (no doubt as an escape from plantations such as that at Pain's Hill), and a wood of conifers may have been something of a novelty. Today the character of this part of the grounds, though still beautiful, has completely changed, and bears testimony to the œcological supremacy of the beech rather than to that of the tribe of conifers of which it was originally composed.

The walks appealed to Price, who at Pain's Hill " enjoyed the dear delight of getting to some spot where there were no traces of art, and no other walk or communication than a sheep-track," while at Claremont " a wood which Rousseau might have dedicated *à la rêverie* is so intersected by walks and green alleys, all edged and bordered, that . . . they act as flappers in Laputa, and instantly wake you from any dream of retirement."

The lake, which is entirely artificial, is about twenty feet above the level of the river. It is thirty-one acres in extent. The present water wheel was manufactured by Bramah early in the nineteenth century; it is of iron, thirty-two feet in diameter, and cost eight hundred pounds. In Hamilton's original wheel, water was conveyed " through a spiral pipe from the circumference of the wheel to the centre of it, from whence it was discharged into a trough," and from there through pipes into the lake.

* *Essay on Modern Gardening.*

C

Interior and exterior views of the Roman bath sheltered by one of the magnificent cedars, for which the park is now noted. Top right, Bramah's suspension bridge across the Portsmouth Road.

Nowadays Pain's Hill is chiefly noted for its trees, and particularly for the cedars of Lebanon, which are to be found on the lawn by the house, on the islands and by the side of the lake, and on the heights above. In 1904 the late H. J. Elwes, author of *The Trees of Great Britain and Ireland*, found one of them to be 115 to 120 feet high and 26 feet 5 inches in girth. He declared it to be the largest cedar known to him in the British Isles.

III—*Pictures* versus *Prospects*

Picturesque gardening, the art of Kent and Shenstone in imitation of Italian scenes, continued to be practised until the end of the century and thereafter ceased to exist. A strenuous battle was fought over its expiring body . . . the struggle between its devotees and those of the naturalist school. At the time, through a confusion of ideas, the devotees of the picturesque were termed the followers of nature and the nature-lovers were known as utilitarians. Of the former, Uvedale Price, country gentleman and amateur gardener, was a fierce warrior in the cause, and, although evincing throughout his writings a love like Rousseau's for " a simple thorn-bush, a hedge, a barn, or a meadow " (Price is accredited with having made a successful imitation of a bye-lane), he was discriminating and sure in his choice of material and possessed a fine imagination. John Payne Knight, who cudgelled by his side, was an " arbiter of taste " and possessed a renowned collection of pictures, which included a selection of Claudes and no doubt influenced him in his choice of sides. Though a fierce and at times unfair critic of Repton, who had taken the place occupied by Brown in public demand on the latter's death, Knight, by the violence

35

of his writing, secured a recognition of the damage that was being done to sixteenth- and seventeenth-century gardens by the ruthless destruction of the landscapists and succeeded in gaining a general re-acceptance near the house of the formal flower garden which had disappeared for nearly a century. This was to everyone concerned so obviously a necessary reform that even Repton was laying out formal gardens before the end of his career.

Of Repton, the chief but always urbane opponent of Price and Knight, there is little to be said that is not already well known. He is still the idol of landscape architects, mainly because he was careful to leave behind him explanations of a simple and adaptable technique and descriptions of easily reconstructed effects, together with ingenious paper slides showing rural scenes before and after " improvement." He was eminently fitted to take on Brown's mantle, and succeeded in obtaining almost as many commissions as his predecessor with only a tittle of that self-confident gentleman's personal popularity. That he was not acclaimed with the enthusiasm accorded to the latter was due to the efforts of his learned opponents who arrived in the field too late to challenge the theories of Brown during his lifetime (though the angry Knight was not above apostrophizing him dead), and succeeded in creating a critical public which took upon itself to analyse and amend designs in a manner hitherto unknown.

Repton, though deploring the practice of picturesque methods in gardens, was yet content to crown his hillocks with temples and scoop out Claudian amphitheatres in the approved picturesque style. It is perhaps unfortunate that he was committed to vague theories of utility and natural beauty, while possessing enough artistic talent to have achieved much more had he been unfettered by them. Peacock sums up the man and his work in the following good-natured caricature taken from his novel *Headlong Hall*. Repton, in the character of Mr. Milestone, has just described to his host the carving of the figure of a giant from a piece of solid rock.

" SQUIRE HEADLONG: Miraculous, by Mahomet !

" MR. MILESTONE: This is the summit of a hill, covered, as you perceive, with wood, and with those mossy stones scattered at random under the trees.

" MISS TENORINA : What a delightful spot to read in, on a summer's day ! The air must be so pure, and the wind must sound so divinely in the tops of those old pines !

" MR. MILESTONE: Bad taste, Miss Tenorina. Bad taste, I assure you. Here is the spot improved. The trees are cut down; the stones are cleared away; this is an octagonal pavilion, exactly on the centre

Bards yet unborn
Shall pay to BROWN *that*
tribute, fitliest paid
In strains, the beauty of
his scenes inspire.

BROWN

KENT, *who felt*
The pencil's power : but
fir'd by higher forms
Of beauty, than the pencil
knew to paint,
Work'd with the living
hues that Nature lent,
And realiz'd his land-
scapes.

KENT

Nor SHENSTONE
thou . . .
Shalt pass without
thy meed, thou son
of peace !
Who knew'st, per-
chance, to harmon-
ize thy shades
Still softer than thy
song ;

SHENSTONE

Knight of the Polar Star !
by Fortune plac'd
To shine the Cynosure of
British taste ;
Whose orb collects in one
refulgent view,
The scatter'd glories of
Chinese Virtu ;

CHAMBERS

REPTON, *who came*
too late to be immor-
talized by Mason, but
he is portrayed in
the character of Mr.
Milestone in Peacock's
Headlong Hall.

REPTON

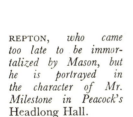

For this miniature gallery of Landscape Gardeners a fitting commentary is found in verses from William Mason's *English Garden* and from his *Heroic Epistle to Sir William Chambers.*

37

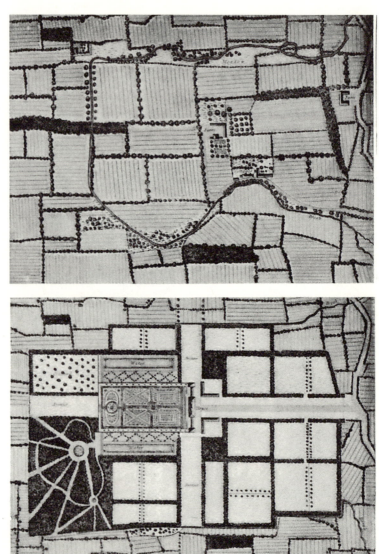

of the summit; and there you see Lord Littlebrain, on the top of the pavilion, enjoying the prospect with a telescope.

"SQUIRE HEADLONG: Glorious, egad ! . . . You shall cut me a giant before you go.

"MR. MILESTONE: Good. I'll order down my little corps of pioneers."

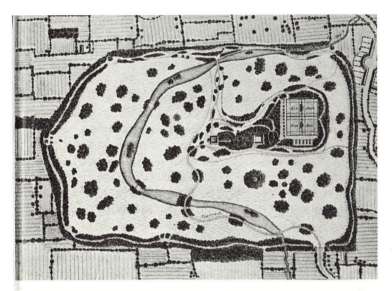

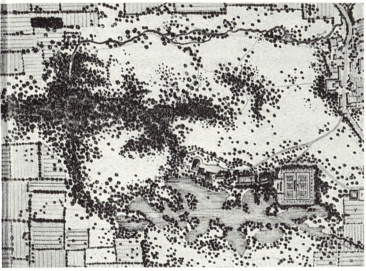

The plans on this and the facing page from Loudon's "Country Residences" illustrate various treatments of a hypothetical site. The first is the site and the second is its transformation into a garden "in the style prevalent about a century ago." The third is in "Mr. Brown's style — generally prevalent at the present day, 1800." Finally, there is shown the same site laid out "in the style of the author, J. Loudon."

This doughty band apparently having been summoned, "the Squire and Mr. Milestone . . . set out immediately after breakfast to examine the capabilities of the scenery. The object that most attracted Mr. Milestone's admiration was a ruined tower on a projecting point of rock, almost totally overgrown with ivy. This ivy, Mr. Milestone observed, required trimming and clearing in various parts;

a little pointing and polishing was also necessary for the dilapidated walls; and the whole effect would be materially increased by a plantation of spruce fir, interspersed with cypresses and juniper, the present rugged and broken ascent from the land-side being first converted into a beautiful slope, which might be easily effected by blowing up a part of the rock with gunpowder, laying on a quantity of fine mould, and covering the whole with an elegant stratum of turf."

Unfortunately for an unseen occupant of the tower, this gunpowder plot turned out to be an only too-emphatic success.

In the years 1794-6, the three participants published their manifestos, of which Repton's *Sketches and Hints on Landscape Gardening* is today the most widely read. Lesser lights, like William Marshall, author of *A Review of the Landscape*, 1795, immediately took sides and the war waged long and fierce. The argument was always the same and revolved around Shenstone's already quoted dictum that gardening should follow painting, and it provokes a smile to read today that at that fateful time of artistic indecision, landscape gardening was solemnly declared by critics in high authority to be " as superior to landscape painting as reality to a representation."*

The issue of the contest took some time to emerge, but at the beginning of the nineteenth century we are fairly safe in saying that picturesque gardening in the old form had in practice disappeared.

It was not an unqualified victory for the " natural utilitarians." Knight, as we know, won his point in the restitution of the formal garden, helped by the warnings of great Romantics like Cowper, Wordsworth and Sir Walter Scott, who deplored the havoc wrought on the national heritage by the Improvers. By the 1840's, under the influence of Nesfield, Sir Charles Barry and Paxton† the wheel of taste has so far revolved as to favour the creation of knot gardens, mounts and straight-lined walks. That it was thought necessary to go back to mediæval gardens for inspiration at this time is a fact of some significance in the light of the phenomenon of Pre-Raphaelitism which burst upon the astonished English public a few years later.

But, in spite of this copyist architecturalism and its growing popularity, " landscape gardening," divorced from picturesque ideals, lacking any organized principles and requiring few qualifications in its practitioners beyond a vague " appreciation of natural beauties " and a few practical abilities, had definitely come to stay.

There are several reasons for its popularity. Chief among them we must count a certain national laziness in matters of art, an in-

* *Observations on Modern Gardening.* Whately, edition 1801.
† See p. 184, *The Picturesque*, C. Hussey. Putnam, 1927.

ability or disinclination to probe beneath the surface or to hark back to origins, which may have made Knight's exposition of his theory of the picturesque a difficult piece to construe. As has been pointed out, there was, too, the growing feeling for nature fostered by Rousseau and the earlier writers of the Romantic Movement, the force of which was so strong as to compel artists to accept the " thou shalt have none other gods but me " attitude which an admission of its principles implied. Also, the effects of the Industrial Revolution were beginning to make

This fountain in the garden of White-knights was designed by Lady Diana Beauclerc. In the words of Mrs. Hofland's book on Whiteknights, from which this engraving is taken, it " affords a fine specimen of the taste that lady so eminently possessed."

themselves felt.* They enabled Cowper to observe, rather sententiously, that " God made the country, and man made the town." Eighteenth-century expansion had raised hideous blotches on the landscape, and to avoid the sight of factory chimneys it was necessary to seek the mountain fastnesses of Wales or Scotland. Thus wild scenery came to be regarded as the finest form of landscape, and men could listen to Ruskin saying in all seriousness that " there may be proved to be indeed an increase of the absolute beauty of all scenery in exact proportion to its mountainous character," and with him be ready to give away the whole view from Richmond Hill " for one mossy stone a foot broad, and two leaves of ladyfern," a remark which many of our present-day rock-garden enthusiasts would heartily endorse.

The world of make-believe in which men like Pugin and Ruskin buried themselves was not conducive to artistic progress. Painting and sculpture became frankly representational, and the Royal Academy, which had given art a certain cachet with fashionable society, was each year crowded with a public eager to acclaim the subject which in approximation to life seemed readiest to step out from its frame. Gardening at this time fared rather differently. As an art it was moribund, but its scientific side was rapidly being developed. Every Victorian gentleman who could afford one possessed a greenhouse in which he cultivated the newest importation from the West Indies and Borneo, where intrepid collectors were

* For an account of the development of the English landscape, with particular reference to economics, see *The English Tradition of the Countryside*, by W. A. Eden, *The Architectural Review*, 1935.

denuding whole forests of orchids to satisfy the latest European craze. They were busy in more temperate climates, too, and their industry resulted in a wealth of new material for the formal gardens that were now reappearing. At home, hybridists were at work. The parent of the moden dahlia, to take but one example, had been cultivated in Europe since 1789, but in 1826 the Horticultural Society was growing sixty varieties, and by 1841 one English dealer listed the astonishing number of one thousand two hundred. Unfortunately, nobody thought of any more original ways of using this material than dotting it about in the landscapist's shrubbery, or embroidering it in patterns on raised beds in the lawn, where the geranium and calceolaria remained supreme for the summer months of half a century.

A garden house from Mrs. Hofland's book on Whiteknights, showing the prevailing taste for rusticity and the romantic outlook on garden design.

This period introduces the practice of planting trees singly, instead of in clumps. Left, a typical example, with which are combined the interlacing gravel paths characteristic of the period. Right, the Long Walk.

A GARDEN LANDSCAPE, 1840

Redleaf, Penshurst

Redleaf was laid out in the first quarter of the nineteenth century by William Wells, amateur artist and Fellow of the Horticultural Society. According to Loudon, " Mr. Wells' operations on the park and scenery at Redleaf were . . . comparatively few, and not such as in any degree tended to alter the character of the place. He widened the river in one situation, and altered its direction in another, in order that it might be better seen from the windows of the house; he removed hedge rows and laid down arable land in pasture, so as to give extent and unity to the park or lawn; he added to or diminished the masses of wood for the same purpose; and he formed a walk so as to enable a stranger to make a general circuit of the place." *The Gardeners' Magazine*, July, 1839.

All this Mr. Wells carried out very skilfully in the traditional manner, but it is not particularly for his landscaping effects that he is accorded a place in our gardening chronicle. Loudon observes:

" Now the great merit of Mr. Wells as an amateur artist is, that, while he has heightened and improved the natural beauties of Redleaf, he has been constantly employed for the last thirty years in creating artificial beauties there, which do not, in the slightest degree, interfere with the great leading natural features of the place. There are very few other proprietors who would not, while improving such a place as Redleaf, have done violence to the natural character of the place, by the evident intrusion of art. . . . The garden scenery at Redleaf consists of a kitchen garden, an orchard, an English flower-garden, a Dutch flower-garden, and an anomalous description of flower-garden, which may be called the rock-garden. This last garden constitutes by far the most singular feature of the place, and is totally different from anything else of the kind in England. The idea of forming it seems to have arisen from the existence of a ledge of rocks in another part of the grounds, and from the abundance of rock, of a kind easily quarried (red sandstone), under most parts of the surface. . . . The suitableness of

[Continued on page 47]

43

View across the Rocky Lawn, showing the Descent of the Rock Walk to the Rocky Hollow.

Rustic Billiard-Room in the Dutch Garden.

On these two pages are recent photographs, beside each of which is reproduced the corresponding drawing from the July, 1839, issue of The Gardeners' Magazine, in which the garden was described. The known accuracy of these sketches makes their comparison with the photographs doubly interesting—a comparison which shows the results of one hundred years of growth. Top right, the Rock Garden, one of the first examples of the " natural" type of rock garden. Bottom, the Rustic Billiards Room in the Dutch Garden, with its modern counterpart in the form of a squash racquets court. Opposite, the English Garden. The floor of the summer house is of irregular oak chunks, the walls are inlaid with varnished woods, and the roof covered with bark cut in the shape of tiles.

English Garden and Summer-house.

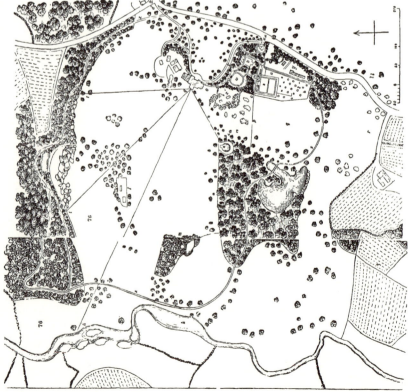

Comparative plans of the grounds before and after "improvement" by William Wells. In the lower plan the river has been widened, a lake formed, and a walk made round the estate. Plantations of trees along the road and drive prevent the view being seen on the approach to the house. The outcrops of sandstone to the north in full view of the house are a key to the character of the estate, which is extremely broken and varied.

*Top left, Land-
seer's seat, from
which there is a
prospect of the
lake. Top right,
a terra cotta basin
on the main walk
round the estate.
Right, a rustic
shelter on the lake
peninsula.*

the stone walk to this rocky garden is worthy of notice—the walk is formed by flat laminæ of the sandstone . . . joined together in the most irregular forms, like the lava pavements in Portici."

From the above, and from the illustrations, it will be seen that Mr. Wells, hovering in the background of nineteenth-century garden art, played a most important part in the development of the rock-garden, of crazy paving, and of rustic work; in fact it is possible that he actually originated one or other of these forms. In these doubtful introductions it would seem that he had a lot to answer for; but in fact his use of them differed from that of the present time. His rock garden was indigenous, and not a Kentish pile of Westmorland stone, nor was his rocky walk degraded into serving as a terrace for the house as is so often the case today. His rustic buildings were certainly bizarre, but still in the picturesque tradition—a rustic Chinese dairy, billiards room and orangery in propinquity to the Dutch garden may be accepted as *jeux d'esprit*. As Loudon says, " the making of the rustic buildings formed a source of amusement to him which was greatly heightened by the adaptation of the crooked branches and roots of trees to the architectural forms proposed." Examples of this craft nowadays are a lamentable travesty of the formal precision and elaborate detail of the remaining structures at Redleaf.

A cottage with Cyclopean stone-work in its lower storey, which must be one of the first known examples of authentic half timbering in the revived Elizabethan style. Circa 1825.

Elevation of a Cyclopean Cottage designed for the Residence of an under Gardener.

For the Victorians, the little gardens strung on the girdle of the path which encircled the estate were of small importance beside those parts of the grounds planned in imitation of natural scenes. Here Mitford and Loudon praised the clever transition from terrace to view, and here the romantic Landseer painted in a rocky glen. Here, too, Douglas, the great explorer, seeing a fine specimen of the creeping juniper, uttered an exclamation of delight, and flung himself down upon it, explaining to his astonished host that he had often spent a night on such a bed, alone in the wilds.

Those who have patience to follow the winding paths of Redleaf, now mossy and overhung with arching evergreens, will notice the wealth of new evergreen trees which gave the later landscapists more opportunities for composition than the earlier practitioners of the art. The cunninghamia, the redwood, the wellingtonia, the Himalayan fir, the Lawson cypress, and many others of the coniferous tribe to be found in this garden, were unknown to gardeners of the eighteenth century. At Redleaf, these superb trees in close plantations impart to the walks that air of solemn grandeur which Pope loved, and Chambers longed for and failed to achieve.

THE XIXth-CENTURY TRADITION

I—*Victorian Ideals*

THE unfortunate duality of temperament with which the Victorian garden was endowed was not an aid to its establishment as an artistic entity. Until this moment there had been no middle course to steer in garden planning—the pre-landscape garden had called for regularity, the landscape garden for irregularity—now there had to be a compromise. The exalted Victorian mind had not yet learned to compromise; in consequence it botched.

And what a glorious, gaudy botch it made ! It will be remembered that Victorian garden-makers were forced to encounter the problem of the villa or suburban plot, admittedly a difficult case even today when the " formal-informal " combination in garden design is accredited with operating so successfully. But in those days the increase in the number of suburban residences with grounds of one-half to two acres simply meant that the landscape garden was represented by a shrubbery and the architectural garden by a " pattern." A cedar of Lebanon, a clump of plumous pampas grass and some pieces of rockwork were used to make a miniature landscape on the front lawn with a crescent moon and stars carved out of the turf for bedding at the back. The grotesque indecency of either act would not have been admitted then . . . it was impossible to make a travesty of nature now that she was a servant, to be bullied with impunity. Amateurs were in fact recommended to arrange their beds by " selecting some part of a pattern of a carpet or wallpaper, or by placing a few bits of coloured paper in the debuscope and then copying the multiple scheme so produced." In this garden for three months in the summer could be seen the result of their rich taste in colour among the half-hardy subjects coaxed from the shelter of the now-popular small greenhouse.

Without doubt, richness was what the Victorians desired, and rich was the effect they achieved. Who cannot respond warmly to the comfortable air of well-being emanating from the succulent leaves of the echeveria or certain of the sedums and sempervivums, plants without whose generous presence the carpet bedding system could never have existed ? As a contrast to the universal prevalence of showy summer flowers, the discovery of this method of leaf-embroidery must have come as a welcome change. In 1878 a writer described carpet bedding as " the latest novelty in flower garden embellishment," and foresaw its great future popularity. The system is still practised in all diligence by the authorities who rule over our public parks.

One would be loth to see these museum pieces disappear entirely and with them the curious plants whose employment in this form of gardening is an excuse for their continued cultivation.

But carpet bedding was not the crowning luxury of the Victorian display. There remained the sub-tropical garden (see tailpiece,

Alternative treatments of a sloping site : the " Natural "
and the Terrace. From Hughes' Garden Architecture.

The characteristic components of the early nineteenth-century garden are illustrated in the frontispiece to McIntosh's Practical Gardener. *Right, rustic work ; the magnification of the individual flower, and the intrusion of the bedding-out system into the landscaped park.*

Above is a design for steps from Hughes' Garden Architecture, *showing debased architectural taste. Overleaf, a view of the gardens at Shrublands, laid out in the Italian manner by Sir Charles Barry and the artist Nesfield, with whom he collaborated on several occasions.*

page 54),which for sheer industry and expense exceeded every known form of outdoor horticultural pursuit. An importation of the 70's from Paris, it quickly became anglicized, and displayed, as well as the banana, agave and chamaerops palm, such frankly temperate plants as Japanese maples, bamboos and berberis. The banana especially called for elaborate protective measures to prevent its broad leaves being torn to ribbons in early summer gales. One important result this form of gardening had—it opened the eyes of the horticultural public to beauty of form and colour in foliage as well as in the flower itself. Since the turn of the century, when carpet bedding and sub-tropical gardening began to fall into disrepute, the ability of the horticultural eye to perceive æsthetic significance in the plant as a whole seems to have considerably lessened.

The mid-nineteenth century saw the arrival of the professor of landscape gardening. This figure was due to put in an appearance at about this time; Repton had been the perfect prototype, and enough literature had resulted from his period to produce in garden architecture the academic mind. Sad to relate, the professor did not make much stir among the English public, who liked their landscapists cast in the John Bull mould, and the academician was sent packing to America, where he flourished exceedingly, set himself up in universities, and is no doubt partly the cause of the general lack of originality to be found in the landscape art of that country today. However, he figures in several English treatises of the 50's and 60's. The professor is entreated to be a man of delicacy, to hide his own feelings so as not to wound those of his employer, to pander to the ladies " who as a rule are possessed of taste in a more marked degree than are men "—in handling the latter he is urged to " yield in trifles, but in important cases present a firm but respectful opposition at the proper time, and at no other "—milk and water tactics indeed compared with those of our autocratic Brown.

Such caution would not appear to have been necessary. With no public appreciation of pleasing shapes or well-connected plans and with a limitless number of styles to draw on for variety, the professor could hardly fail to please. He was at liberty to draw diamond-

shaped beds for the terrace to the early Gothic house and barrel-shaped ones for the Elizabethan, with the satisfaction of knowing that he was working in an approved style. Occasionally details such as the correct number of steps in a flight were apt to worry him, and he had to remember in a small stairway to make the number uneven so that the ascent or descent might begin and finish with the same foot. Vases were another source of trouble, for although there were plenty of examples of the classic urn, it was almost impossible for a Gothic vase to avoid resembling " an octangular egg-cup, a wine-glass of rude pattern, or a font." It was even considered doubtful whether a Gothic building or terrace would in any case permit a vase as an accessory. But apart from such details the professor led a carefree and industrious existence, rigorously imposing the principles of a new style in the gardens of a rising class of country gentlemen. The

The increasing interest in flower cultivation as distinct from garden lay-out was an important influence in the development of the mid-nineteenth-century garden. Above, a dahlia : " Brilliant " : from Hibberd's Amateur's Flower Garden.

new Gothic pleasure-grounds did not in fact admit of much frivolity in decoration; they were as barren as the current conception of Gothic architecture. Slopes were allowed to take the place of balustrades: " crenellated copings are admissible, but will be found rather heavy. Yew and box hedges will suit well . . . the well-shaven bowling-green is eminently suited to domestic Gothic; so is the ivy bed, ivy mound or ivied wall." All very monkish; but if you happened to possess a veritable Gothic garden like that of the Byron family at Newstead

Abbey you could always enliven it by the addition of a French, a Spanish and an Italian parterre and Gothicize this mélange with the pointed balustrading which enclosed it. You had the unimpeachable authority of the architect of the new Houses of Parliament (whose Italian tour had been no less profitable than that of Addison, " the first Victorian ") to dabble in whatever style you chose. Or, in the words of another designer:

A suburban garden lay-out from Hughes' Garden Architecture, 1866.

" The modern architect may build a house in the classic or in the Gothic style; or he may adopt the historical and geographical variations

53

of these styles, as exhibited in the Hindoo, Elizabethan, Italian, English, and other manners of building. In like manner, the landscape-gardener, who would lay out grounds at the present day, may adopt either the oldest, or geometrical style . . . or he may adopt the modern or irregular style in which the forms of nature are brought into immediate contrast with the forms of art; and he may, further, combine the two styles in such a manner as to join regularity and irregularity in one design."*

O glorious epoch, in which Hindoo and Italian contribute equally to the national style ! How many present-day designers can claim such enviable versatility ?

* P. 17, *The Villa Gardener*, J. C. Loudon.   London, 1850.

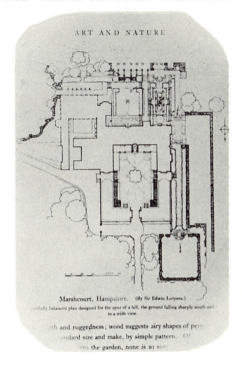

ART AND NATURE

Marshcourt, Hampshire. (By Sir Edwin Lutyens.)
...tifully balanced plan designed for the spur of a hill, the ground falling sharply south and to a wide view.

...th and ruggedness; wood suggests airy shapes of pe...
...ndard size and make, by simple pattern. ...
...nto the garden, none is so su...

II—Colour and the Cottage Garden

Followers of the mid-Victorian style of gardening, complacently accepting the incongruity of their creations in the old landscape parks, and the architects who had made Italian gardens at country seats like Shrublands in Suffolk, were rudely awakened from their contented dozings by the publication of William Robinson's *The English Flower Garden* in 1883. This work contained Miss Gertrude Jekyll's views on garden colour.

The æsthetic values of colour had concerned eighteenth-century garden makers but little. Kent and his followers had dabbled in questions of light and shade, but remained faithful to sombre reds and browns and the golden shades which lit the glowing Claudian sunsets; when the introduction of new and showy flowers made the subject one for urgent consideration, the matter was ignored. At first, those plants which were brightest were considered best, much as the gaudiest toys are cherished in the nursery. Until their novelty wore off, geraniums, calceolarias and lobelias, representing the most vivid tones

55

of the three primaries, were the favourite bedding subjects. The notions of colour blending and of colour stimulus in pattern, more familiar to us today, were indirectly fostered by the camera, when painters like Sargent, whose technique consisted largely in " seeing with the camera's eye," discovered that the apparatus recorded effects of light which could be reproduced in painting by judicious combinations of the light-reflecting pigments. The palette was split up into a hundred different shades, many of which had hitherto been considered " muddy " or drab but were now found to be necessary for successful imitation of the camera's vision. This idea resulted in the degenerate derivative paintings which even today adorn the walls of the Royal Academy and the covers of chocolate boxes, but it also made way for the experiments in colour forms which enabled constructional painters like Cézanne and original romantic painters like Van Gogh to assume the significant positions they hold in the history of modern art.

What colour did for gardens is another matter. It enabled Miss Jekyll, the first horticultural Impressionist,* to translate gardening straight into terms of painting, viz.:—

* Francis Jekyll's memoir of his aunt recalls that she retained throughout her long life a profound admiration for the French Impressionists and that an illustrated book on the subject was a source of enjoyment during her last winter.

The style of the cottage garden was a reaction from the ornamental carpet bedding characteristic of the Victorian period, which still persists in the lay-out of municipal gardens. The floral clock from the Princes Street gardens in Edinburgh is a " tour de force " in this type of design.

Heading the reaction against Victorian formalism are the gardens of William Robinson and Gertrude Jekyll. Perhaps the most characteristic feature they evolved was the herbaceous border. This example is at Millmead, Bramley. The house, commissioned from Sir Edwin Lutyens by Miss Jekyll, she intended, together with the garden, as an example of what could be made of a narrow site.

"Should it not be remembered that in setting a garden we are painting a picture—a picture of hundreds of feet or yards instead of so many inches, painted with living flowers and seen by open daylight—so that to paint it rightly is a debt we owe to the beauty of the flowers and to the light of the sun; that the colours should be placed with careful forethought and deliberation, as a painter employs them on his picture, and not dropped down in lifeless dabs, as he has them on his palette?"

So we return to pictures, but this time in search of a technique rather than an ideal. Impressionism,* fifty years old and in process of being discarded by painters, seeks a new home in the garden.

And thus, with the help of Robinson, the herbaceous border came into being. The author of *The English Flower Garden* in a protest against formalism, demanded large beds of simple shape and the use of hardy flowers, which he advocated in a long chapter on " waste," together with the abolition of fancy edgings, as making less demands on the gardener's time than the popular system of bedding out. He ridiculed the formal " decorative " style of design, and prophesied that " reform must come by letting Nature take her just place in the garden." This was not to be brought about by " reproducing un-cultivated Nature " but by selecting such of Nature's material as seemed compatible with the romantic tumbled aspect of the English cottage flower border. In the cottage garden which had remained unchanged through the centuries, Robinson found material as in-spiring as that which Burne-Jones and Rossetti discovered in mediæval manuscripts and the paintings of Gozzoli. " I am never concerned with Claude," he says, " but seek the best expression I can secure of our beautiful English real landscapes, which are far finer than Claude's," forgetting perhaps for a moment that it was from the works of this painter among other sources that the English landscape had sprung.† In his eagerness for a native as against an adopted

* The contemporary problems which have developed directly as a result of late nineteenth-century concern with this subject are dealt with in a subsequent chapter.

† It is still not generally recognized that some of our famous national landmarks and " beauty spots " (examples are Chanctonbury Ring on the South Downs and the wooded valley of the Thames at Goring Gap) are not spontaneous phenomena, but results obtained by eighteenth-century landowners working in the landscape tradition.

"No one having seen a Lutyens' house of the early period will deny that the ac-companying garden by Miss Jekyll is suited to it." A pro-duct of this famous collabora-tion : Fisher's Hill, Woking, Surrey.

Italian style, Robinson was as active in the garden sphere as William Morris (the father of the Arts and Crafts Movement) in the field of industrial art, and, in a similar way to that in which we now look upon Morris, in spite of his extreme and often reactionary views, as the link between nineteenth-century industrialism and the modern movement, we may regard Robinson as the unwitting link between the old and the very new in garden design.

The pioneers of palette gardening also revived the wild garden, claimed to have been advocated by Bacon,* though in the " heath " or wilderness of his essay he had not pictured the type of flowery meander which present-day landscape architects set about conjuring from oak woods. This most ephemeral of garden styles, the apotheosis of naturalism, offers all the charms of escape for those who pursue this policy in their waking lives—the type (as exemplified by Miss Jekyll in her nephew's memoir) which prefers animal to human society and deplores the advance of science and of civilization. In the wild garden they are in fairyland. As a style it is something of an anachronism today; in the past, however, it has provided the milieu for useful experiment concerning the adaptability of plant life to particular conditions.

The lasting value of the work of William Robinson and Gertrude Jekyll lies in their establishment in popular favour of the hardy plant. Both were gardeners, unlike the planners that had come before; garden-making for them had to be tempered with respect, with curiosity and with experiment. They were pioneers in the art of adapting living material to the site, as indeed they had to be to illustrate their favourite dictum that planting should appear to have " happened " rather than to have been artificially planned. No one having seen a Lutyens' house of the early period will deny that the accompanying garden by Miss Jekyll is suited to it—an opinion confirmed by the equal value of house and garden as manifestations of the vernacular style. The garden in this famous collaboration is thus the perfect adjunct to the house. That, one might think, is a very good reason for its being unsuitable for a modern house, but as yet in this country no alternative to the " colour garden " has been devised.

The end of the nineteenth century was not without its planners,

* The writings of Spenser, Bacon and Milton have provided material for corroboration of the arguments of landscape and " formal " enthusiasts alike, who sometimes forget that these magicians of the written word in their descriptions of delectable gardens were often concerned with more-than-earthly scenes—the unobtainable paradises to which men can only aspire in dreams. Small wonder that here all tastes can find perfection !

although these could scarcely be called of a revolutionary turn of mind. They consisted of a few architect garden planners, who fought the natural school in a manner reminiscent of the battle of the same period at the end of the preceding century . . . Milner and Robinson taking the place of Brown and Repton, and Blomfield heroically donning the mantles of Price and Knight, from whose writings he had drawn freely for his methods.

But the publication of Reginald Blomfield's *The Formal Garden in England*, to which Robinson's book was in the nature of a reply, although springing an attack on the degenerate nature-copyism of the day, did little to stem the flow of public opinion towards the wild and rock type of gardening which is still with us.* In the light of modern experience it is a redundant work, showing a devotion to formalism more dogmatic than were the opinions of its opponents on naturalism, and so it partly defeated its purpose, but many of the author's remarks on the absurdities of the landscape school remain extremely apposite:

" The word ' natural ' can only mean something belonging to nature, or something done in accordance with nature's laws, as, for instance, planting a tree with its roots underground instead of upside down; but when the landscapist uses the word ' natural,' as when he calls his system a ' purely artistic and natural ' style, he means by it a style which imitates the visible results of natural causes, as, for instance, the copy of a piece of natural rock in a rockery. Now there is nothing more natural, properly speaking, about this than there is in the formation of a grass bank in the shape of a horseshoe. In fact, this vaunted naturalness of landscape gardening is a sham; instead of leaving nature alone, the landscapist is always struggling to make nature lend itself to his deceptions."

Compare Croce:

" The artist sometimes has naturally existing facts before him in producing the artificial instrument, or physically beautiful. . . . From this comes the illusion that the artist *imitates nature;* when it would be perhaps more exact to say that nature imitates the artist, and obeys him. The theory that *art imitates nature* has sometimes been grounded upon and found sustenance in this illusion, as also its variant, more easily to be defeated, which makes art the *idealizer of* nature. This last theory presents the process in a disorderly manner, indeed inversely to the true order; for the artist does not proceed from the extrinsic reality, in order to modify it by approaching to the ideal; but he

* The new generation of landscape gardeners now had the overwhelming novelty of colour blending to increase the strength of their already popular arguments.

proceeds from the impression of external nature to expression—that is to say, to his ideal—and from this he passes to the natural fact, which he employs as the instrument of reproduction of the ideal fact."

Blomfield's main object was to obtain recognition of the house as the dominating factor of the garden lay-out, a point of view perhaps to be expected from an architect.

June border in a cottage garden in Essex, planted in the manner of the late nineteenth-century colour-planners.

In this he succeeded, and today this once vexed question does not occupy our attention. It should, however, be noted that it is possible to create beautiful gardens without houses, as witness some of our loveliest parks, in which architecture is only incidental. These, of course, display the very type of art at which this author cavils. One cannot forgive him for his ridicule of the founders of the landscape movement; he has passed by the more important of the eighteenth-century contributors to the art of garden design—the theorists of Sharawadgi,* for instance, who had no faith in mathematics and deified irregularity; who found beauty in infinite variety and treated natural material according to that material's own potential organic pattern. No such lively philosophies as theirs influenced the garden art of his own age, which has prolonged itself in melancholy fashion to the present day.

---

* This word is described in the long Oxford Dictionary as being " of unknown origin; Chinese scholars agree that it cannot belong to that language. Temple speaks as if he had himself heard it from travellers." The following are some of the rare references in literature:

Sir William Temple, *Gard. Epicurus*, Misc. II, ii (1690): " The Chinese . . . have a particular Word to express it (sc. the beauty of studied irregularity); and where they find it hit their Eye at first sight, they say the Sharawadgi is fine or admirable."

Pope, Letter to Digby, August 12, 1724: " For as to the hanging gardens of Babylon, the Paradise of Cyrus, and the Sharawaggi's of China, I have little or no Ideas of 'em."

Horace Walpole, Letter to Mann, February 25, 1750: " I am almost as fond of the Sharawaggi, or Chinese want of symmetry, in buildings, as in grounds or gardens." Letter to Earl Strafford, June 13, 1781: " Though he was the founder of the Sharawadgi taste in England, I preached so effectually that his every pagoda took the veil."

See also *William Shenstone*, by A. R. Humphreys, Cambridge University Press, 1937, pp. 40-41.

An early modern English house by Professor Behrens, at North-ampton. The conventional dry wall and circular steps which form its garden setting are left-overs from the vernacular period and fail entirely to harmonize with the character of the house.

III—Science and Specialization

The present-day garden, with the sixpenny novelette, is a last stronghold of romanticism. T. E. Brown's poem, "A garden is a lovesome thing, God wot . . .," which leaves Edith Sitwell "with a feeling of having been hit over the ear, with no excuse and without provocation," is still successfully assailing less sensitive organs than hers. But, as F. L. Lucas has pointed out in *The Decline and Fall of the Romantic Ideal*, science is destroying the Dryad. The fairy ring has proved to be the work, not of fairies, but of fungi; and though science has restored in some measure that which she has taken away by giving us a new and more substantial mythology, she is being beneficially ruthless with the old methods and styles. Just as the design of the locomotive, the aeroplane, and, for that matter, the modern house, is being changed by scientific invention, in a similar way science will transform the garden of the future. The latter must necessarily be influenced by new materials and their methods of application—for example, by plant importation and hybridization, and the amelioration of soil and weather conditions. One of the chief results of applied science in this field has been to reduce the size of the purely utilitarian sections of the plan. New methods of intercropping (adapted from those of France and Holland) and new prolific yet compact and disease-resisting varieties of vegetables have helped in this process; in the orchard, experiments with dwarfing stocks now enable twice the number of apple trees to be planted in a given area and on suitable soils to produce fruit in half the time that our grandfathers had to wait before obtaining crops of equal quantity. And who except the connoisseur will now plant varieties of apples and pears to keep up supplies for the table from August to May, knowing that from overseas comes fruit as fine, if not finer, than his own carefully wrapped and stored specimens? Heaven forbid that the apple, pear or peach should ever disappear from our gardens (and in their decorative use it is unlikely that they will), but experiments with gas storage and speedier transport may yet reduce the cultivation of the English kitchen garden to an occupation for epicures, and its area to the size of a pocket-handkerchief. Similarly, economic necessity has reduced the size of gardens as a whole. An example of this is the splitting up of large estates into small units for building development; these in turn become specialist plots, where the cultivation of the newest varieties is pursued with an eye to triumphs at the flower show. Thus, since the nineties, when the flower itself took the place of the flower garden in the popular imagination, we have all become gardening specialists.* Proportion, line and balance of colour and form have on the whole little interest for us; we are preoccupied instead with soil, aspect and irrigation. In this manner the rise of scientific horticulture has involved the partial eclipse of garden planning.

Planning goes on, of course, but in what fashion? A great deal of thought and ingenuity is put into the making of rock gardens, those hybrids which derive partly from the eighteenth-century grotto and partly from the Japanese hill garden, but which nowadays are planned from studies of natural Alpine formations. These grotesques call for skill in their creation, but, being entirely representational, contribute nothing to art.† We are not yet in possession of the artistic integrity

* The number of nurseries specializing in one family or in closely related groups of plants—*e.g.*, lilies, heathers, irises, roses, succulents—is a sign of the times, as is also the growth of specialist societies. The following are among those holding regular exhibitions in London: Alpine Garden Society, British Carnation, Rhododendron, Iris, Cactus and Succulent, British Delphinium, British Gladiolus, National Dahlia, and National Rose.

† It has lately been recognized that alpine plants can be cultivated most efficiently in a less prodigal terrain than the " natural " rock garden.

which might enable us with equanimity to use rocks in the manner of the Japanese, nor, apparently, are we blessed with the imagination of a Pope, who decorated his grotto with shells and sparkling stones for their intrinsic beauty and associative qualities. So awed are we by nature that, were it suggested to us, we should be afraid to use a shell as decoration in the garden because such an object is not typical of mountain, marsh or meadow scenery, and our ideas of what is fit for ornament out-of-doors are correspondingly restricted.

Specialization has provided us with heather gardens and autumn colour gardens, developments since the time of Robinson, whose best-known work was published before the brilliant Japanese maple had been recognized as hardy enough to plant in the open border. The latter form of gardening has been particularly encouraged by the large number of new shrubs from Asia and America, such as species of the genera *Berberis* and *Acer*, which have been introduced to this country by explorers like Farrer, Forrest and Ward. It has transformed October from the ignominious position of a dead month on the horticultural calendar into one of the most brilliant of the gardener's year.

All these horticultural developments have only been cursorily treated by garden planners, owing perhaps to an inability to view the garden in the round instead of in its details. The planning of the contemporary garden most often resolves itself into an unsystematized diffusion of parts without the sharp definitions in the planting necessary to coherence in the whole design. The segregation of plants, in both small and large gardens, is an important factor for obtaining this quality of " hanging together," and as such it is regrettable that it is not generally recognized. But even a reform in this direction could not redeem the irrelevance of much contemporary planning or the ineptitude of some units of the garden plan to perform the functions required of them.

Until a general conception of the garden without boundaries can arise in this country the small garden will remain the English problem. " The English garden, like the English Sunday dinner, is pretty much the same throughout the country. Most gardens consist of rose beds, herbaceous border, lawn and rockery, and, in all but the very smallest, there is a pergola garlanded with rambler roses."* This seems to indicate that there is at any rate a uniformity of opinion in the gardening world regarding the components of the plan, and, except for the possible wish to reform the rockery and clothe the pergola with plants less aggressive than the Wichuraiana rose, few will quarrel

* Jason Hill, in *The Gardener's Companion*. Dent, 1936.

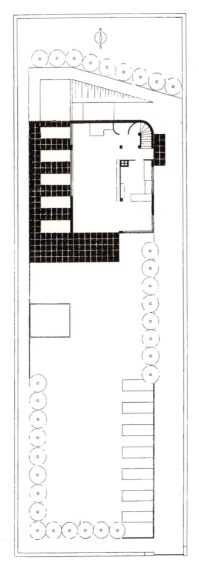

*An example from Belgium designed by
Jean Canneel-Claes, showing the tendency towards simplicity which identi-
fies this type of garden with the
modern house. Above, and right,
plan and two views of the garden
architect's own house near Brussels.*

with such a selection of units. The rose grows to perfection in most parts of this country; the herbaceous border, or, perferably, the mixed border of shrubs and herbaceous plants, is an economical and decorative substitute for nineteenth-century bedding out; the lawn is our most valued legacy from the landscape gardeners, and the pergola, hardly necessary in this variable climate for the provision of shade, fulfils a certain purpose in accommodating those climbing plants which demand good cultivation, training and support. To Mr. Hill's list must be added the modern equivalent of the shrubbery, which is now almost the first thing required of the landscape architect in even the smallest garden.

If there were the same uniformity apparent in the disposition of these accepted parts of the garden, though this would make for a stereotyped formula of design, it would perhaps be a better thing for the English garden as a whole. It is seldom that one sees a pergola serving some logical and useful purpose in the garden scheme, linking up the house and the garden shelter, for instance, or providing necessary height as a background to an architectural garden of flat colour.

Even the lawn is often badly handled. The " open centre " treatment of small gardens will have to become more widely known before the lawn as an entity, the essential *laund* or land, can come into its own. It is a common enough experience to find herbaceous borders or a bedding scheme cutting across a wide expanse of grass in obedience to the architect's dictum that there must be a vista line from the sitting-room window or garden door. What reasons he can put forward for advocating this confinement of the eye between prodigious lengths of flower bed it has not been possible for the author to discover. In nine cases out of ten, treatment such as this results in a crowded plan and the complete elimination of the lawn as a satisfying unit in the design. " I think a plain space near the eye gives it a kind of liberty it loves," wrote Shenstone, " and the picture, whether you chuse the grand or the beautiful, should be held up at its proper distance." This is a possible precept for even the smallest gardens, where borders and walks can be kept to either side, allowing the view from the main front of the house to be of mown turf, unbroken save at its edges where the flower plantations encroach, ebbing and flowing away into distant unexpected corners. The living-room window and garden door may still have their focal points, but these will probably now be set toward the far boundary and need only consist of a marked balance in the planting to arrest the eye and hold it momentarily without enslaving it. Such a garden gains immeasurably in apparent size and repose and loses nothing in dramatic effect. The lawn becomes its main feature, the central body from which depend the limbs of the garden scheme, and though not all sites lend themselves to this treatment (a steeply sloping garden, for instance, may require much terracing and little lawn) it is a safe one for the small garden in this country.

This method of approach is not put forward as a cure for the present ills of gardens, nor is any one formula either wise or practical as a method for design. As Shaw puts it, " Consistency is the enemy of enterprise, just as symmetry is the enemy of art." The use, however, of a method similar to that outlined above, as a mechanical basis for the construction of suburban gardens with rectangular or well-defined boundaries, might help to avoid some of the errors of overcrowding and the loose relation of parts which characterize the vast majority of gardens all over the country. But even if a working formula could be obtained, it would be next to impossible to apply a similar set of rules to the planting of such a garden. Here lies more opportunity for error than in any Minoan labyrinth.

If, then, a new garden technique is to be evolved, it need not necessarily reject the traditional elements of the garden plan, although it is the author's opinion that necessity will drive us to find new forms in which these elements will largely be discarded. Rather, its aim must be to infuse them with new life. Their evolution has been traced through the past two hundred years, and it has been found that it is not the parts in themselves that have been lacking in intrinsic value, but the conception of their makers that has varied through the ages and put them to strange uses. Other units may be added as they become necessary (the tennis court and swimming pool are additions of the last fifty years), and neglected ones, such as the croquet lawn, may be discarded when their time of usefulness is past.

Those which are designed for use are the most important and in some ways the most interesting parts of the garden of today. Perhaps this may be a clue to our enjoyment of the gardens of the future. The hard angularity of the tennis court, with its inevitable wire surround, is a new problem in gardens, and one that must either be solved by relating it to its surroundings, or by giving the surroundings a character in keeping with this new garden form. The swimming pool, so frequently lined with glazed tiles, strikes an unaccustomed note of light and colour in our placid English scene, which since the time of Chambers has lacked entirely the quality of exoticism. Both these elements, designed for use, are uncompromising in their demands upon the artistic structure, and certain it is that the new chord that has been struck must eventually be echoed by all notes in the garden scale, if they are not to be drowned in a welter of strange cacophony. " Something more animated, more significant and more in sympathy

67

with speed and movement will be needed," says a modern writer,
"a type with sharper interests—more up-to-date in the sense that
a modern house is up-to-date." This will call for a new simplicity in
gardens if there is not to be a period of horticultural *Art Nouveau* such
as occurred in the field of architecture and decoration before the present
forms evolved. In the Scandinavian countries there are signs that
the new garden is already establishing itself and in the places where it
is most needed. There, the functionalism of garden schemes for
workers' dwellings and blocks of flats is directly the result of a whittling
down—evidence of the need for the creation of the maximum recreative
area in the minimum space. As an element inseparable from the
problems of housing, and urban and rural development, garden
planning can, with the least opposition, achieve its modern form.

*The garden terrace of a house near Halland,
Sussex. Architect: Serge Chermayeff. Landscape Architect: Christopher Tunnard. The
sculpture is by Henry Moore.*

TOWARDS A NEW TECHNIQUE

I—*Functional Aspects of Garden Planning*

The modern garden architect has as much to discard as had the painter, sculptor and architect of a decade or two ago. He is faced with the necessity of ridding himself of so many comforting, if worthless, technical aids in planning that very little can be left to guide him. He must therefore evolve a new technique as a basis for contemporary garden planning.

In the previous chapters the main influences on garden design have been analysed in relation to problems of the past; now and in the following pages it is proposed to examine as fully as possible the three sources of inspiration the modern designer has at his disposal—those of "functionalism," the oriental influence and modern art—and to endeavour to devise from them three methods which can be co-ordinated or synthesized into a working æsthetic for landscape design. These three methods, which we can term functional, empathic, and artistic, could provide the necessary background for a modern technique. It is possible that the modern garden will arrive by other means than those which the writer is about to discuss—the modern spirit in design is, or should be, a way of thinking and feeling rather than a ready-made formula for achieving an effect—but it would be a mistake to imagine that even the freest forms of planning are not based on unalterable laws and systems of values, and since we are faced with finding a new set to satisfy contemporary needs it can do no harm to suggest some obvious possibilities.

The first of these three influences to be considered, then, is that which is exerted by what has been generically termed the doctrine of "fitness for purpose." The form of art which is architecture has been marked in this movement by a return to functionalism, a principle which demands simplicity and clear statement in planning.

Now a great many people who write about gardens and most of those who make them will say that this happy result has been obtained. The following extract is a typical example of the attitude towards garden planning of well-informed persons today: " . . . Only with the present century, so one likes to think, has that just alliance of interesting detail, coupled with broad and simple lines, untrammelled by particular style or fashion, been achieved."* But is this really so ?

* *The English Country House*, Ralph Dutton. Batsford, 1935.

Variations on an architectural theme. The garden at Hyères by Gabriel Guvrekian, above, with its focal sculpture by Lipschitz, now a decade old, was the forerunner of several similar gardens; an English example near Bristol, opposite page left, by A. E. Powell. In the garden of the Villa Schultz, Switzerland, right (architect, Ernst Mühlstein), brick-built flower-boxes lend an architectural balance to the architect's composition.

Unfortunately it is not. Style and fashion still cling to the " interesting detail " and the " broad and simple lines " of most contemporary gardens. There are few places where the Italian, the Oriental, the Rustic, the Tudor or the Alpine curiosities are completely banished. And what fashion has ever swept and held a country so thoroughly as that for the natural rock garden during the last thirty years in England ? One feels that the " broad and simple lines " are too often employed in the service of axial planning much as they were under Italian influence at Holkham and Kedleston in the eighteenth century; the Italian tradition of the axial vista, revived by Victorian architect garden planners ninety years ago, has not yet been discarded, although it is a pompous anachronism which has had its day. Unfortunately one cannot agree that the contemporary garden is " untrammelled by particular style or fashion "; the influence of classic shapes and idioms may be seen in the designs of ornamental pools and swimming baths all over the country. And what does the author mean by " interesting detail " ? Can it be the romantic gesture to the past embodied in the Italianate lead figure on its pedestal, the classic urn or the well-turned balustrade ? Surely it is truer to say that wherever we look in the conventional garden of today we shall find the styles influencing both the method and the matter of design.

Let us hear what le Corbusier has to say about the academic tradition:*

" The styles are a lie.

" Style is a unity of principle animating the work of an epoch, the result of a state of mind which has its own special character.

" Our epoch is determining, day by day, its own style.

" Our eyes, unhappily, are unable yet to discern it."

* Translated by Frederick Etchells.

71

Garden for a week-end house at Cobham, Surrey. The land is frankly planned as a playground and for low upkeep cost. A combined swimming-pool and boating lake is flanked by a sandy foreshore for sunbathing. All original trees remain on the site and new planting consists of flowering shrubs and waterside plants. This house and the houses in the two illustrations on pages 74 and 75 were designed by Raymond McGrath. The gardens illustrated on pages 72-76 were designed by the author.

What, then, is the twentieth-century substitute for the " Styles " ? As long ago as 1897 we find the Austrian architect Adolf Loos writing: " The lower the standard of a people, the more lavish are its ornaments. To find beauty in form instead of making it depend on ornament is the goal to which humanity is aspiring." For Loos beauty in a work of art was attained by the completeness of its utility and a high degree of harmony of its parts—a view which followers of the modern movement have not yet seen fit to alter.

Thus the doctrine of function in modern art is accompanied by a fresh conception of form. How much importance this latter factor

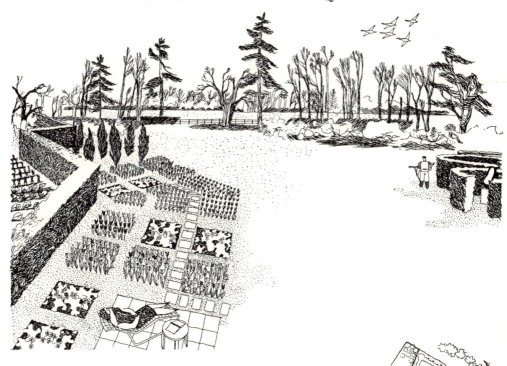

Geometric shapes in a garden at Walton-on-Thames. To the left a combined rose and tulip garden leads to a walk between flowering shrubs which borders the entire plot (about an acre in extent). A hedge divides the garden proper from a kitchen garden running alongside the road. Asymmetric as opposed to central axial planning saves the main lawn area from unnecessary sub-division. To the right are circular spaces enclosed by hedges designed for the display of sculpture.

should be given in landscape planning is a debatable point; here it is sufficient to say that the poets of pure form in architecture, like Wright and le Corbusier, have accepted it as a sufficiently strong foundation for the new way of building.

While the appreciation of pure form is the basis of æsthetic satisfaction in architecture, the other arts are not very differently inclined. Painters, with the exception of one notorious modern group, no longer point a moral finger and are content with patterns of line and colour; in some cases with the pattern only. Sculpture becomes the rhythm of plastic form in relation to an expressive medium. Music belongs

73

again to mathematics.   And the industrial arts, in which artists are
at last allowed to speak, become the complement of all the others in
economy of form, trueness to material and relation to contemporary
living.   The relationship between the arts has become closely knit, as
in all previous great periods of artistic endeavour.   Yet the art of
gardens has remained so far aloof from this combined activity.
Clearly it is in need of the invigorating modern spirit.   The sculptor
and the painter once participated in gardens; nowadays they are thus
outside, in spite of the fact that the best of modern sculptors are designing for open spaces and the painter's conception of form and colour
is essential to a modern appreciation of garden planning.

The fact that garden making is in part a science does not free it
from the duty of performing an æsthetic function; it can no more be
turned over to the horticulturist than architecture to the engineer.
That it has a place beside the other arts is more than clear from a study

*An architectural garden, part axial, part asymmetrical, at St. Ann's Hill,
Chertsey. Screen walls frame the distant views. A sheltered position allows
many half-hardy subjects to be grown, including cordylines and the chamaerops
palm. The sculpture on the right of the sketch is by Willi Soukop.*

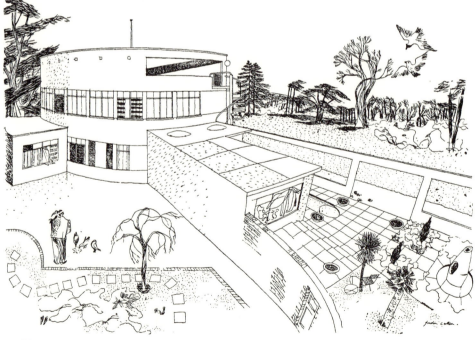

of the past, and that it still has a mission to fulfil is, in the light of the demands of contemporary life, an obvious reality. We need gardens for rest, recreation and æsthetic pleasure; how, then, can we neglect the art that makes them rational, economical, restful and comprehensible?

This last adjective is the key to our solution of the problem of landscape design for the future. Understanding cannot be complete unless the pieces of the puzzle fit, and where house and garden, dependent on one another now as always, are maladjusted, æsthetic comprehension is impossible. The modern house requires modern surroundings, and in most respects the garden of today does not fulfil this need.

It will be apparent from what has been said that the modern garden should be the logical outcome of the principle of economy in statement and the sociological necessities which have influenced modern archi-

A garden for a country house near Leicester. The view from the principal rooms extends over a circular plunge pool and ha-ha and across thirty miles of typical shire landscape. The enclosed garden on the right is planted with alpines and dwarf shrubs set in flat beds between alternate squares of grass and paving. Local stone is used in the construction of the retaining walls and steps.

75

House and garden near Halland, Sussex. Except in the immediate surroundings of the house the arrangement of the beds and borders is of a non-architectural character. Irregular "atmospheric" plantations of flowering trees and shrubs link the house to the landscape. In common with all the other examples in this series of sketches, the house and terrace command distant views, yet, as can be seen, the framing of these views has been carried out differently in each case. The architect of the house is Serge Chermayeff.

tecture. As we have seen, once in its history at least architecture has followed the lead of the garden makers; today it is the turn of the latter to learn the lesson of the modern way of building.

The functional doctrine of planning has, in fact, made some headway among a few isolated groups and individuals practising the art. The following are extracts from a paper submitted by the President of the Swedish Garden Architects' Association at the first international congress of garden architects held in Paris in 1937. The full significance of this paper lies in the fact that it was a group effort and not the product of any one individual's ideas.

" The utilitarian style has strongly influenced the construction of domestic buildings; they are often asymmetrically planned, have large windows exposed to the sun, and, if possible, are sufficiently free from screening to permit of distant views.

" Ordinarily, the garden is planned in such a way as to form a direct relationship with the house, access from one to the other being everywhere facilitated. The garden thus becomes a part of the dwelling. Its arrangement is decided more for the activities of people —especially of children—than for flowers. It allows for seats and benches resting on paved areas which relate to the house, and lawns as extensive as possible, though not always mown. Paths and walks are reduced to the minimum and often consist only of stepping stones between which grass or creeping plants are allowed to grow, thus conserving a homogeneity between the units of the plan. Pools for the children are much appreciated and, when possible, they are made deep enough to allow for bathing. In general, trees are not numerous in these gardens; most people prefer to have flowering shrubs. When herbaceous plants are used they have a definite part of the plan devoted to their culture, and need not, as formerly, be confined to the conventional flower bed. There is little room in gardens now for the bedding plants which for so many years have enjoyed such a wide vogue.

" The utilitarian style of building has exercised a profound influence on gardens, which it appears to be ridding of conscious symmetrical planning. The arrangement of gardens is freer and more mobile than formerly. One does not look for axial construction and the monumental planning of former styles, which could never be prevented from looking severe, above all when close to the house, the hard lines of which can be softened by subtle plant arrangements. One strives to create a contrast between the disciplined outlines of terrace walls, paved spaces, pools, etc., and a free and luxuriant vegetation designed to produce a happy decorative effect and to give the impression that it is a work of nature or of chance. It is pleasant to leave an existing gnarled pine in a paved courtyard the aspect of which is otherwise strictly architectural, or to arrange matters so that trees with heads of interesting shapes appear to detach themselves from the smooth walls of the house, their rigidity being softened by the foliage. It is admissible that between the paving stones of courtyards space should be left for isolated plants to give the impression that they have grown there spontaneously."

These passages provide a clear view of the break with tradition which has taken place in Swedish gardens since the advent of a rational architecture in the Scandinavian countries. The styles, axial and symmetrical planning, ostentatious decoration—all this rhetoric has been discarded to make way for the simple statement. Only one stumbling block to future progress seems to lie in the path of these clear-headed pioneers. From the last extract quoted it appears that the romantic conception of Nature has not been entirely swept away. This acts perhaps only as a qualification to their statement. The influence of a wild and beautiful countryside which has played its part in creating the new technique is still too strong to loosen its hold. It is, however, unfortunate that for the Swedish garden architect the spontaneous intrusion of Nature into the garden scene is not enough, and that she must still be eulogized as the immediate inspirer of effects which are the creation of man's own artistry.

Nature worship, commendable enough in its rational aspects, suffers from an almost universal romantic interpretation which in the past has proved dangerously stultifying to the free development of garden design. It is therefore all the more alarming to see that this cult, in its most romantic form, has been embraced whole-heartedly by one of the foremost of town planners.

" I shall place this house on columns in a beautiful corner of the countryside; we shall have twenty houses rising above the long grass of a meadow where cattle will continue to graze. Instead of the superfluous and detestable clothing of garden city roads and byways, the effect of which is always to destroy the site, we shall establish a fine arterial system running in concrete through the grass itself, and in the open country. Grass will border the roads; nothing will be disturbed —neither the trees, the flowers, nor the flocks and herds. The dwellers in these houses, drawn hence through love of the life of the countryside, will be able to see it maintained intact from their hanging gardens or from their ample windows. Their domestic lives will be set within a Virgilian dream."*

The dreams of Virgil can be said never to have included a vision of modern woman getting her feet wet in the long grass, but le Corbusier must be congratulated on extending the natural garden style to its logical conclusion. Few people want to be condemned to languish at a window and exercise exclusively on a roof garden. Yet, to the author quoted, the levelling of a space for recreation† in the long grass of the meadows and the banishment of the flocks and herds would seem to be a sacrilege and certainly a desecration of the contours of the virgin soil. The sportsman with his gun can take his pleasures in purely agricultural country, but most of us soon find that Nature

* *Precisions*, le Corbusier.

† In other works, notably in *The City of Tomorrow*, le Corbusier emphasizes the need for humanizing the surroundings of his buildings.

House by le Corbusier at Poissy, " rising above the long grass of a meadow " (see the quotation from le Corbusier's writings on page 78), provides an extreme example of the natural garden, though it will be observed that in the background some attempt at the humanization of the surroundings has been made.

unadorned (even with the alternative of a roof garden* by le Corbusier) is not enough; that the landscape, or at any rate the surroundings of the house, must be planned in accordance with human needs. Certainly the old conception of the garden designed as a series of pretty pictures must be put aside and a new and economical technique be used. The garden as an organization, whether that organization be only a path and a plant, must exist and can be ordered into a perfect and satisfying relationship with the house and the landscape.

A recognition of the importance of the plan as an organizing factor would help to make this functional garden planning a reality. The plan as co-ordinator must be translated into its three dimensional terms—those of plane, line and mass, the first denoting spatial values (open and closed areas), the second linear values (lines of communication, division, etc.), and the third mass values of inanimate and living material. That which is necessary in such a planning system automatically becomes that which is good and the need for space filling or accentuating decoration disappears. The designer thus confines

* In Stockholm, where the roof garden was introduced in tenements for workers, it has largely been discarded since it was found that the tenants showed a marked preference for the gardens which surround the buildings.

decoration to the integers of the plan, whose functions will determine their form. This does not mean that his initiative will be restricted; on the contrary, he may claim, for instance, the right to use all available plants in a given scheme, or he may decide to employ only one. He is no longer bound by the conventional necessity for picturesque representation, and looks upon the imitation of Nature as a long-perpetuated artistic fraud. He shakes off the academic yoke of the styles, free to interpret the message of his work of art in a new and more forceful manner. The functional garden avoids the extremes both of the sentimental expressionism of the wild garden and the intellectual classicism of the " formal " garden; it embodies rather a spirit of rationalism and through an æsthetic and practical ordering of its units provides a friendly and hospitable milieu for rest and recreation. It is, in effect, the social conception of the garden.

Model of a garden at Liedekerke, Belgium, which has been planned to preserve the view from the house and for economy of upkeep. It shows an appreciation of the sculptural quality of plant material and an asymmetrical arrangement of the plan units which are distinguishing characters of the few sympathetic gardens for modern houses.

II—Asymmetrical Garden Planning

It will be necessary in the following chapter to consider the second source of inspiration for the modern garden—the Oriental influence—but first it will be advisable to discuss the technical device of asymmetry which was borrowed from the Orient in the eighteenth century and gave rise to the " irregular " landscape garden. It has rarely been used to liberate the formal garden from its conventional rigidity. These so-called " formal " gardens, in which planning has not been influenced by the existence of natural phenomena or the exigencies of use (architect-designed caprices of the academy), are usually symmetrically planned. This has not always been so; in the Middle Ages the unsymmetrical garden, " that strange and recondite set of fancies," was often the accompaniment of the feudal dwelling. Evelyn was the first Englishman to use the word " asymmetry "—he was discussing the town planning of London—but in his writings also occurs the first mention of the words " vista " and " canal," those essential characteristics of the axial, symmetrical gardens of the *Grand Siècle*. In spite of the intervening occurrence of the landscape garden (which significantly arrived from China on a porcelain vase by way of Tivoli and Cooper's Hill) symmetrical planning returned with the increased use of perspective by painters and the Italianate revival in the nineteenth century. Only today with the death of the culture which lauded the axial vista, that most snobbish of all forms of Renaissance planning, has the cult of symmetry begun to suffer a deserved eclipse.

If we analyse designs of most gardens planned on the axial system, we find that the common practice is to make the right side of the plan repeat the left; that is, right and left balance on a vertical axis, which is inversion and the most usual form of symmetry employed in gardens.

Towards the end of the last century there was a breaking-away from the stocking of symmetrically arranged groups of beds with plants placed in rows and geometrical patterns—carpet-bedding and bedding-out. One or two designers declared that the stiff lines of the borders produced a sufficiently " formal " effect to warrant what they called a more natural type of planting; thus herbaceous borders came into being, and one occasionally saw an old box-edged garden being planted with shrubs, herbs and colonies of bulbs. Planting became asymmetrical, but the lay-out of this type of garden has remained in the old state. One might go as far as to say that 90 per cent. of

F

A contrast in garden plans : right, the gardens of the Villa Lante, Bagnaja : Italian axial planning of the sixteenth century ; facing page, the Alcazar, Seville : occasional symmetry in the parts but not in the whole. A product mainly of the same century.

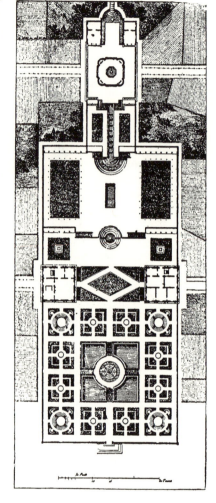

so-called "formal" gardens are created on this rule, which has been, and probably will continue to be, an eminently safe one for any cautious designer to follow.

The remaining 10 per cent. of "formal" designs are based on the system of double inversion, or balance on a diagonal axis. Such plans resolve themselves into states of single inversion if viewed from certain angles, but where this form of balance is consciously used care is taken that the effect of diagonal balance shall be apparent where it is needed. Such designs are not symmetrical, but are nevertheless well balanced, although more delicately than those which rely on a vertical axis. Their æsthetic appeal lies indeed in the fact that their special form of balance is less easily recognized.

The next step, taking us still further from symmetry, and into a new field of conscious exploration, reveals the existence of a form of balance which has been termed "occult." It is essentially a relative quality depending on the interplay of background and foreground, height and depth, motion and rest, but as such it can be reduced to a science and obtains through all composition in art and nature. Primitive peoples have always been responsive to its urge. The native whose scanty attire consists of a flower placed over the right or left ear is relying on the artistic effectiveness of asymmetry against a strictly symmetrical background (what more obvious example of symmetry than the human face?), an arrangement which does not destroy balance, but serves to accentuate it.

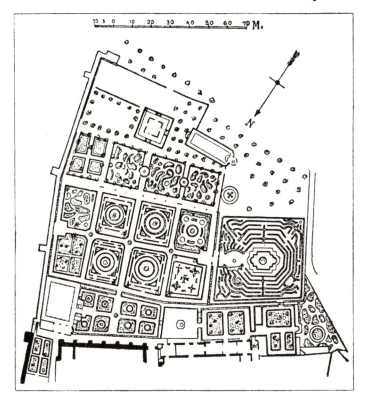

This form of balance often requires the steadying influence of a frame or boundary. In the plan illustrated of a Japanese garden of the Yedo period it is clear that the screen of fencing which defines its limits is an aid to balance rather than a detraction from it. There is a force of opposing movements in this plan which the boundary serves to control.

" Occult " balance deserves more investigation than it has so far received from landscape designers if our gardens are to keep pace with modern developments in architecture. It must not be imagined, however, that " occult " balance and asymmetrical compositions in general are being advocated here as having any special merit above the more usual kinds of order and arrangements. Each has its value in a different sphere. The use of asymmetrical principles is being stressed for a good reason. We are searching for a new technique for the contemporary garden, for a garden designed to be a complement of contemporary architecture, which embodies to a large extent the

83

principle of asymmetrical balance. This is not shown by all good modern examples—it would be a loss to architecture if symmetry were frowned on—but it would be neglecting a wide field for experiment to remain content with the old axial and symmetrical conception of garden planning when a form directly in sympathy with modern æsthetic needs is asking to be employed. Neither should it be thought that we are impinging upon the old and vexed question of the architectural garden versus the landscape garden. The asymmetrical technique, essential to the latter, can be applied with equal success to geometrical compositions, and in fact to any part of the garden plan.

One of the reasons for a Western fondness for symmetry in gardens (we must except the garden art of certain ages) has been the unimaginative use of asymmetrical principles where they have been applied. The landscapists adopted irregularity without giving proper consideration to its necessary complement, texture. This, a sensory quality, and distinct from pattern, which appeals only to the eye, is not necessary in symmetrical garden compositions; in fact, an elaboration of plan may destroy the effectiveness of the design. Texture, or at least some stimulus to the tactile sense, is an essential of the irregular " landscape " garden, which must always have a three-dimensional form and demand an esoteric kind of appreciation. The appeal of the irregular garden must necessarily lie in its subtlety. It goes without saying that the regular garden of the past possesses an appeal of equal importance, though of different character. The garden made by Le Nôtre for Louis XIV at Versailles, for example, appeals to us not so much in its subtlety as in its perfection of detail. Gardens such as this, true works of art, exhibit the symmetrical technique in the highest form it can ever attain. The sweep of the terraces and avenues at Versailles is in the nature of a broad classical gesture, the product of an intellectual age. Yet the neglected asymmetrical technique embraces the delicate nuance as well as the bold impression. It is symbolic of the plastic arts of our own time.

We seek again a rationalism, but a more evocative expression of it. Our modern buildings are simple statements, but our gardens have a new mission—to fulfil the need for an affinity with Nature which Louis never felt and which even Rousseau could not have imagined. In an age which has divorced itself from the life of the soil we need Nature's materials (not her image)—her sticks and stones and leaves, the stimulus of her proximity. We like to throw our windows open to the sun and to see it filter into our dwellings through the branches of a neighbouring tree, or to hear rain falling softly on the foliage. We begin (it is only a beginning) to use Nature as the Oriental has for

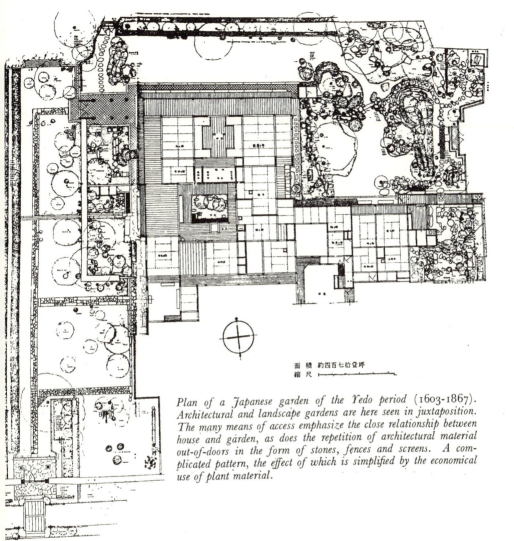

面　積　約四百七拾坪
縮　尺

*Plan of a Japanese garden of the Yedo period (1603-1867).
Architectural and landscape gardens are here seen in juxtaposition.
The many means of access emphasize the close relationship between
house and garden, as does the repetition of architectural material
out-of-doors in the form of stones, fences and screens. A complicated pattern, the effect of which is simplified by the economical
use of plant material.*

centuries, not as a refuge from life, but as a sustainer of it. And that
is why, in our search for sources of inspiration for a modern planning
technique, one of our journeys must be, not to Byzantium or the Near
East, where symmetry was once abandoned, but to the Orient itself
and the old gardens which developed round the capital of Heian.

This journey should be no mere borrowing expedition, but rather
in the nature of Gauguin's to the South Seas or a modern sculptor's
imaginary pilgrimage to an African village. There is no need to
linger on the Mediterranean seaboard—Gertrude Jekyll brought back
a sufficiency of ideas from that quarter—and we can pass by the
mystical temple gardens of India. Even China's symbolical landscape

*A modern Kyoto garden.   Vegetation controlled, but not abused.
The trunks of the trees in front of the house have been trained
to their present angles and the low azalea bushes to shapes
required of them by the rhythm and movement of the composition.*

gardens with their islands of eternal youth and happiness—scenes
which provoked a century of Nature-copyism in the West—hold little
for us.   They are too far removed from our material conception of the
universe.   It is to the gardens of Kyoto that we must turn, some of
them centuries old, but all possessed of a secret which only intimacy
with Nature can reveal.   The individual garden, except as an example,
need be no concern of ours, but an understanding of the principle
which lies behind it must be achieved if we are to enlarge our artistic
horizon.   It should be added that not even a superficial attempt is
being made here to explain the Oriental attitude to art in general,
and that only a very brief indication is to be given of the Japanese
attitude towards garden art in particular.

  For at least a century and a half Kaempfer was the only authority
on Japan, and except for his book, which was published in England in
1726, the artistic isolation of that island from the Western world was

unbroken until the eighties of the last century. Since then we have seen enough of the trappings of Japanese art to sicken us of it for ever, but the original landscape art of that country has never been clearly understood by European garden makers and only rarely by painters such as Whistler, who found economy of line and colour in the Japanese print. In the domestic arts, modern architects of the calibre of Wright, Miës van der Rohe and Corbusier acknowledge a debt to the native building, in which a remarkable unity exists between the nature of architecture and its materials. It is important to note here that the same unity exists between the nature and forms of Japanese garden art.

Until recently the little that has been borrowed from Japanese art has been its ornament in painting, in architecture and in gardening. In gardens, who is not familiar with enthusiastically conceived imitations of the tea-garden, with their ubiquitous stone lanterns, torii, shrines, and summer-houses ? Oddly enough, imitators have seized upon the least important aspect of Japanese art for the exercise of their zeal. It is well-known that the excessive use of ornament is an idea repugnant to the Japanese, who choose black or grey material for the roofs of their houses, in contrast to the bright red of the Chinese, and to whom gilded dragons are an exotic fancy. As one modern writer has put it, the Japanese come at the beautiful by way of the necessary. They live in rooms empty of furniture and display their articles of virtu in the *tokonama*, a simple wall-recess which takes the place of a frame. The modern American and European house is approaching this ideal through the increasing use of built-in furniture and fitments, and the relegation of the contents of the bulging Victorian curio cabinet to the more restrained background of a glazed niche in the wall.

The phenomenon of Japanese art most significant to modern designers should be the feeling for a spiritual quality in inanimate objects, that feeling which makes the Oriental smile at an European painter's efforts to obtain physical likeness and exact perspective. Long before the days of the Impressionists, the Japanese artist was painting the iridescent mountain mists and finding in the curve of the rocks and the sweep of the waterfall a sensation akin to that aroused by his own aspirations and activities. The waving of a branch in obedience to the wind, the refreshing and purifying flow of a surging stream—these things were significant to landscape painter and gardener alike, and were loved by them as being near to their own experience.

There is a parallel in this attitude with some of the more recent manifestations of contemporary thought. Without elaborating the point in too much detail, it may be said that a sense of personal identification with Nature and with the flow of the creative forces of the

universe is expressive of the beliefs of some of our modern philosophers, whose individual and personal mysticism would seem to spring from the same root. For centuries European art has turned its back on the fundamental conception of Nature in art, and Western man has imagined himself and Nature as being in antithesis. In reality, his much-vaunted individuality is an illusion, and the truth which the Orient now reveals to him is that his identity is not separate from Nature and his fellow-beings, but is at one with her and them. And until the European has learned to cultivate the empathic attitude and has discovered that apart from the symbolism of the East and behind it is an æsthetic antithetical and complementary to his symmetrical classic conception of composition, the universality of art can never become an accomplished fact.

This conception of Nature and natural forms finds one of its expressions in Japan (and is beginning to in Europe) in the unity of the habitation within its environment. This is accomplished in more than one way. Japan has for long had a genius for building. The typical Japanese house is an example of great skill in the use of native

materials, the management of space and the distribution of rooms. It differs from, say, the pre-war English house in being almost one with Nature. In warm weather the house becomes part of the garden, the sliding paper screens, which keep out the cold blasts and snow of winter, being easily removable so that the whole side of the room may be thrown open to let in the cool summer winds. Since the advent of steel frame construction—that is, for the last fifty years—it has been possible to build houses in this way which conform in other respects to European standards, but it has not been thought necessary to do so in England until the present time, when, with the advent of the modern house, experiments in this direction are being carried out. The sliding - folding window may help to break down the rigid barrier between house and garden both here and on the Continent, where the cumber-

89

some and costly device of disappearing windows, only possible where basements are constructed, has hitherto held the field.

In Japan, another method of achieving the coalescence of a building with its surroundings is the province of the landscape architect. The house walls are echoed by screens placed near them, stone repeats stone on the simple terrace, plants encroach on the walls of the house and wreath themselves among its timbers. Yet all is restrained, calculated and under control. No great waves of vegetation beat upon the building; man shows his respect for Nature by allowing her admission to his scheme of planning, but sees to it that the respect is mutual. He permits no uncalled-for display of exuberance. In return, he does not exploit his plant material. The chief criticism which a Japanese has to make of our European gardens is against what seems to him the barbaric massing of colour to be found everywhere. As has been truly said, until recently we have regarded the grouping of colours as one of the most sublime of human arts. Now, while the trend in all art is slowly moving towards an acceptance of form, line and economy of material as being of first importance, some of our gardens are beginning to show signs of this change of view. In Japan, colour in gardens is used sparingly and backgrounds are always studied closely. Extreme simplicity of effect is sought. The grouping and arrangement of plants is of far greater importance than the colour of their flowers. Endless trouble is taken in the training of trees, especially the favourite pine, so that their shapes may gain a particular character which is necessary to emphasize some special effect. Many gardens may be almost without flowers, yet full of interest provided by the variety of the shapes of the trees, their arrangement, the grouping of shrubs, shadows, reflections in the water, and other subtleties evoking in the onlooker sensory and intellectual pleasures such as a lavish display of colour in itself could never arouse.

To create this atmosphere their feeling for inanimate Nature has made the Japanese supreme in such matters as the placing of stones, the management of contour lines and the use of water. Eleven centuries of practice in the art have not dulled perception, and some of the newest gardens are of the greatest refinement and subtlety. They are as different from the originally imported naturalistic gardens of the Chinese T'ang period as art can make them. Except in rare cases there is no attempt made to imitate natural scenes either in miniature or on a life-size scale, a popular and quite erroneous impression of Japanese gardens current in the West. All the important gardens are products of a highly stylized art in which experiment is encouraged and conventional repetition avoided.

90

When the sentimental, superficial approach to this Oriental art through its merely decorative aspects has been abandoned by the Western mind it will be discovered that the underlying principles may very well serve as part of the basis for a modern technique. Obviously, our own must be founded on broader considerations, since it is governed by other factors. In general, the Oriental likes to enjoy his garden sitting down; our habit of " going for a walk " does not in the least recommend itself to him as a method of appreciating its qualities. Our own gardens are planned for active enjoyment, not for purely meditative purposes, and it is necessary to arrange them so that they are pleasant to live in as well as to look at. In all spheres of modern art creation is increasingly demanding identification with the social problem, and garden art, though at present sadly retrograde in this respect, must soon embrace the communal idea or cease to function as an integral part of modern life. But the new technique, as we have seen, demands many of the special qualities which make the fundamentals of Japanese landscape art significant as a modern example. The appreciation of form and texture which combine to create unity between architecture and its surroundings is not the least of these qualities. We have not yet learned to apply it success-fully in the West. The Japanese grasp of rhythm and accent in plant

The familiar English attempt to adopt garden ideas from Japan is the " period " Japanese tea-garden fashionable during the second half of last century. Right, a wistaria arbour and tea house on the lawn at Bagshot Park. Below, in contrast, a modern garden in Leicestershire which adopts an æsthetic principle from the Japanese instead of merely borrowing the superficial style. Water, stones and planting are linked intelligibly to the small pavilion.

91

arrangements far excels our own, as does the marshalling of detail
into significant and relevant patterns. It is the æsthetic conception
which is the foundation of this virtuosity that must be allowed to seep
into our artistic consciousness. Let us absorb the Oriental æsthetic.
By doing so we shall help to rid ourselves of individualism in art and
gain identity with art and life.

Men-an-Tol, Cornwall.

III—Art and Ornament

If the conception of the garden as a work of art is a difficult one to accept, it is because, in this country at any rate, garden designing has for so long been regarded as a craft. The revolution in gardening taste which took place in the eighties with the popularization of the hardy plant and the commencement of the second stone age, with its plethora of flagged paths and dry walls, enabled every man to be his own garden maker. And not only every man, but every woman who, before Gertrude Jekyll donned her famous gardening boots, had wielded no implement more formidable than the garden scissors, now enthusiastically embraced the new "hobby." Since then we have had an age of picture-book planning. Pandered to by nurserymen, horticultural journalists and contractors, the public has had its way with gardens, and the elimination of the artist from one of his most useful spheres of influence has been the inevitable result.

It would be wrong to suggest that the garden has been killed with anything but kindness, but dead it is—stone dead, in fact—and when the art of gardens is revived it will not be in many respects similar to much that has passed in its name during the last fifty years. A far greater affinity will probably be apparent between the first landscaped gardens of two hundred years ago and the freely planned landscapes of tomorrow, which, made possible through the operation of very different economic and social laws, will embrace garden, town and countryside in one unfettered whole.

It would be pleasant to think that when the landscape artist is allowed to return to the garden he will bring with him the inspiration, if not the active co-operation, of the graphic and plastic artists, who will be instrumental in forming his own taste as well as that of the age in which he lives. For although it is true that gardens, like buildings, can be complete in themselves without mural decoration or sculpture, it is necessary that the significant forces which find liberation in painting and carving or modelling shall also be expressed in the complex technical achievement which is the garden artist's manipulation of living and natural forms. As a parallel, the best of contemporary architecture is closely related to the best of modern sculpture and constructivist painting because architects, sculptors and constructivist painters are in written or personal contact with one another.* (This is as it should be: the way of one progressive artist must eventually be the way of another, although their means of expression may be different. Such a phenomenon is not a result of copyism, but of collaboration, and springs from a similarity of purpose.) To achieve works of art of similar importance, the landscapist must be a collaborator in this movement, although at first he will have more to learn than to teach. The painter can open his eyes to the interrelation of forms, plane and colour values more forcefully than ever in the past, when, in the eighteenth century, landscape gardeners learned from the Italian masters, and, in the late nineteenth century, garden colour planners from the Impressionists. The sculptor can convey to him the new feeling for texture and masses, the need for working outside his medium as well as in it, and the necessity for an unrestricted experimental technique. Much as the sculptor derives inspiration from the form and quality of the material he uses, the garden designer can consider the site and its features as the arbiter of his planning. The present-day rule is to adapt the site to fit the designer's technique, and not the technique to fit the site, as should surely be the case. The high-handed treatment of natural features which is involved in the former process is frequently explained and lauded as showing man's domination over Nature, but more often than not this acts as a justification for employing a set formula of design which is the technician's excuse for being an incompetent artist. Such traditional formulas must go, and the maxim, " Failure is to form habits,"† become the garden designer's only fixed rule. The true artist knows the possibilities

---

* See *Circle*, published by Faber and Faber, 1937.
† Walter Pater.

Sculptured and " Interpreted " Wood. Left, figure by Zadkine in Edward Wadsworth's garden at Maresfield Park.

Below, the Paul Nash " object " referred to on page 100.

and the limitations of his material. The true garden artist learns to co-operate with Nature, and, while not becoming a slave to her demands, is content to let her express his meaning in the simplest yet most convincing manner. Only thus can there be perfect harmony within the work and between it and its surroundings.

A step in the direction of a new technique for garden planning could be made by discarding the academical theory of decoration as mere surface trim-

95

ming in favour of the structural decorative methods that are being applied elsewhere.

Not long ago Adolf Loos wrote: " *Evolution der kultur ist gleicheb-deutend mit dem entfernen des ornaments aus dem gebrauchsgegenstande. Ich glaubte damit neue freude in die welt zu bringen, sie hat es mir nicht gedankt* " (" Progress in taste goes hand in hand with the elimination of ornament in everyday things. I hoped by this discovery to bring new happiness to mankind, but nobody has thanked me for it "). Elsewhere he says that there is no need to regret our inability to create new forms of ornament; that we have progressed beyond the need for such sedatives.

Here we have stated simply and concisely what is a natural consequence of the contemporary movement in architecture and its emphasis on " function." Applying this credo, ornamentation has in itself a suggestion of disguise, of what is, in fact, a tangible form of lying, and that the decoration of useful objects is a confession of failure in their original design.

Familiar examples of this dishonest practice abound in our domestic surroundings: radio and gramophone cabinets are dressed up to suggest the customary drawing-room whatnots or cabinets for *objets d'art*; electric light globes and gas heaters to imitate candles and log fires. These are perhaps not always so much confessions of failure, however, as manifestations of snobbery. It must be plain that any progress in taste in designing useful objects must be towards making them not only functionally as perfect as contemporary scientific knowledge will allow, but also beautiful in themselves. And this is happening as often as the contemporary designer is being given a place in industry.

This sort of ornamentation has not been so apparent in gardens, yet one would be happy to see knobs and finials removed from garden seats and a simpler substitute for the florid wrought iron gate, a relic of medieval craftsmanship. Most garden ornament of today is, in fact, something in the nature of a gesture to the past; sundials, well heads, lead tanks, Italian stone benches, millstones, antique statuary are anachronisms which, when good in themselves, are not necessarily anything worse than sentimental passages in the composition of the garden. Their fault is that they have ceased to mean anything and they have become too familiar to evoke in the spectator more than a casual polite interest. As ornaments they merely clutter the landscape and can perhaps be discarded. That which takes their place should be modern in spirit and design. Seats, gates and vases of simplicity and usefulness and sculpture by artists who create essays

A Figure of a Nymph in the Hofgarten at Bayreuth. A study in natural and artificial forms.

in form, and not decorative pastiches, are already proving their excellence.

This problem is also complicated by the fact that garden backgrounds—and in the case of sculpture that is particularly apparent—are usually themselves of a heavily ornamented nature. Because of this, the use of conventional figures to terminate vistas and as centres to flower gardens may very well be incorrect. The advice of Shenstone to set statues in the valley as an answering note to the balustrading on the hill shows more discrimination—there the figure could be appraised apart from a complex background of foliage which might lessen its interest. Sculpture, which relies for its appeal on intricacy and subtlety of detail, is best placed in relation to plain undecorated surfaces such as walls, level lawns or water. This usually calls for an

G

asymmetrical placing which may or may not invest the composition with romance—anyone who has seen the waterside figures in the *Hofgarten* at Bayreuth will know how excessively romantic an air even mediocre sculpture can be lent when divorced from any architectural influence—but the point to be made is that in highly conventionalized and elaborate settings the intricacy of even the best modern work may lose its full effect. If we are still to have long vistas with " focal points," we shall find that they are better provided with simple terminals like stone columns or non-representational and geometrical forms in stone, concrete, metal or wood.

" Long vistas are better provided with simple terminals ". . .
A fountain in Hopton Wood stone by Willi Soukop.

MODERN INTERPRETATIONS OF TRADITIONAL FORMS

Top left, a painted mural decoration forms an engaging background to a garden devoid of colour in its planting.

Right, a drinking fountain in the courtyard of a school in Stockholm.

Bottom left, vegetable sculpture. Ivy on a wire frame in André Vera's garden at St. Germain-en-Laye.

Right, plants behind bars. Treillage decoration in a garden by Charles Moreux in Paris.

It is necessary to eliminate many of the representational attributes of garden sculpture. To be arresting, to force the onlooker's attention to some aspect of formal unity in the world around us, is the function of all works of art. Even the self-sufficient Dr. Johnson was heard to remark: " We cease to wonder at what we understand." A garden figure which is a faithful reproduction of the familiar has, in fact, become a cliché. The form should arouse our curiosity, should emphasize some aspect of Nature which will set spinning the wheels of conjecture or of fancy. It is only in this way that garden ornaments will acquire fresh value.

This much, then, we can say for certain: that ornament is only legitimate in situations that require it and in such form as will add to the experience of the beholder.

If naturalism is to go, what, besides non-representational sculpture, is to take the place of our posturing figurantes and Barriesque boys, those regrettable descendants of the nymphs and fauns that sported at the Leasowes ? We have said that the placing of sculpture may be asymmetrical and that it is, in fact, shown to best advantage in this way, and that the conventional placing in centres and focal points is often wrong unless simple abstract forms are employed. How else, then, is the evocative note which hitherto has been voiced by ornament to be obtained ?

In the author's opinion, the cost of good sculpture, with the exception of mass-produced cast concrete figures from sculptors' models, will always work against its deserved use in gardens generally, and it therefore behoves us to search for new material. This becomes a question primarily of seeing with new eyes, or with the eyes of the imagination. We find that there exists in certain movements today a tendency to enlarge the term of artist to include those who in imagination can form a composition or even recognize in certain material objects concrete symbols of subconscious desire and imaginings. Thus it can be said that the imaginative observer can develop his latent sense of form, and as no two people will find the same object significant in the same way, we must expect a great many unconventional and widely deviating phenomena to be selected. Paul Nash, for instance, in an article on the " Object,"* illustrates a curiously twisted and gnarled piece of wood, which, upright in a setting of stones, conveys a significance equal to that of a sculptured form.

Even more familiar material can be found for the garden. One large stone of interesting shape is worth the multitude which form the laboriously made " natural " strata of a present-day rock garden.

* *Architectural Review*, 1936.

The writer has found that an emotive effect can be produced by placing stones in settings where their formal qualities can be appreciated in relation to near-by masses—at the bases of dwarf concrete walls on granolithic paving, for instance, where a spreading stone may in its implied movement assume the tense immobility of a large toad waiting for flies, or as isolated and grouped objects in grass at the edge of thin woodland, or by water. These arrangements are the antithesis of so-called " natural " rock groupings which are invariably commonplace and superficial forms of decoration. People who dislike this " formal " placing of natural stone are invariably those who are unaware of the incongruity of the crazy paved terrace as a surround for the Georgian house or the ornamental well-head as a fitting decoration for any situation today.

But by far the widest field for symbolic representation is provided by living plant material. As an ornament near water, what could be more expressive and complementary than the weeping willow? Those plants which by their familiar or grotesque form attract our attention are sometimes equal to sculpture in emotive value. We might be content with far less than we ask in garden decoration were we but able to cultivate an empathic attitude to our material. The qualities which we can appreciate in plants either for their formal qualities or their element of grotesqueness are valuable for a complete appreciation of the garden scene. Even the geometrical shapes of topiary, when presented in unconventional arrangements, will be seen to have acquired a meaning apart from their associations with the past.

There is still a need for applied decoration in gardens, but to what degree we find this necessary depends largely on our ideas of what is suitable as decoration in itself. Further, if it is to be of value, such decoration must avoid superficiality and bear a direct relationship to its surroundings.

The surfaces of the walls and floors of the garden offer opportunity for decoration where ornamentation in the sense of three-dimensional sculpture would be impossible. In English gardens for many years we have been accustomed to see patterns in stone paths or paved areas made with granite setts or brick, and tile and stone let into brick walls and piers for decorative effect. Glazed and figured tiles we seldom see, mosaic almost never; our climate is not considered suitable for these, and in many situations this is correct. There is, however, scope for their employment on walls and in covered loggias where they have as yet scarcely appeared. These materials are familiar to us in gardens of warmer climates and have had their share of praise at one time or another. In these pages the task is to present the problem of decoration in terms of contemporary design.

The architect in presenting us with the modern house leaves to the landscape architect a difficult problem in designing a suitable setting. Although pleasant in other surroundings, the familiar dry walls and stone terraces spouting with every conceivable rock plant obviously disturb the skin-smooth texture of certain modern house elevations and their effect of simplicity. Recently this incongruity has been excused by a writer on landscape architecture on the grounds that the use of local materials in its immediate surroundings provides a contrast to the " foreign structure " raised above them. The weakness in this argument, which is in any case a far from sympathetic one, is that contrasts can only be contradictions unless they are contrasts in kind, and achieved between forms or materials which bear some relationship to one another. In the case of the modern concrete house and the dry wall there is a distinct incompatibility between the ideals of the age of engineering and one of the last remaining expressions of a century of arts and crafts. It should be stated, however, that the modern house is far easier to relate to its surroundings when constructed of more familiar materials.

There is no artificiality where there is no attempt to disguise materials. Most concrete paving aims at being a substitute for stone; the deception is encouraged even in the laying, when crazy or random courses give a path or terrace of this material an ill-concealed air of inappropriateness in any surroundings. The concrete paths in the illustration overleaf do not pretend to be other than they are; the texture and shape of each slab is as precise and formal as a machine—there is no attempt to make them appear natural—so they achieve a condition of fitness for purpose and, with this, integrity of form. The surface of this paving was treated with carborundum at the floating stage partly to prevent slipperiness in wet weather and partly for the sparkle which this material imparts in sunlight. A form of decoration such as this in which convenience plays an important part is a more than sufficient justification of its use in the modern garden. The vases illustrated are cast in reconstructed stone, essentially a rough-textured concrete composition. Their decoration lies in their texture, colour (a soft cream), and in the incised lines which form part of the design.

Glass may soon return to gardens, as it has in the past. The early eighteenth century saw glass used in grottoes, and even Repton was known to employ mirrors in his pavilions to reflect the landscape. Looking-glasses might well find a use on the face of walls to mirror

An architectural garden in which granolithic paving has been used as a groundwork. The incised division lines were cut at distances no greater than two feet apart to prevent cracking. Concrete walls colourwashed a pale green retain the small exotic garden on the upper level.

the garden in miniature, now that weather-proofing of this type of glass has achieved perfection, but this form of mural decoration does not exhaust its possibilities. The comparatively new glass brick, while not suitable for free-standing construction without a frame of concrete or metal, may in future help to make the garden house a place of light and warmth rather than of gloom and chill, as it so often is. There will be no further need for dark corners in the garden when these bricks become inexpensive enough to use in places where light is needed for plant growth, and no need for draughts when glass screens come to be regarded as decorative as well as useful components of the terrace.

In Herr Miës van der Rohe's garden pavilion the effect is heightened by the contrast of bright metal columns. In many forms metal is more suitable for certain structures than wood, brick or stone. The conventional brick pergola, for instance, with its more than sufficient columns, might well be replaced by tubular metal arches where lightness and grace are desirable. The long-forgotten Victorian iron arch

103

Above, a garden house by Miës van der Rohe. The black glass walls reflect with curious depth the pattern of the surrounding water garden. Left, a glass screen in a garden designed by Harry Maasz. It helps to shelter tender plants but does not exclude light.

still stands in some old gardens as a testimony to the charm of simple light construction.

The list of new materials and methods can never be exhausted if experiment becomes part of the technique of the modern landscape architect, one of whose employments must be " to study the relations between the evolution of garden art and that of the other arts under

104

contemporary conditions, as well as the part played by scientific materials and methods in these evolutions."* The use of modern sculpture, significant objects, plant forms and new decorative materials which are decorative in themselves has been touched upon here, and the value stressed of a return to the imaginative conception of garden decoration, a conception which was lost almost at the beginning of its magnificence in the middle of the eighteenth century. The twentieth-century garden will be reborn when the imaginative attitude is again adopted. Then, as in the Oriental landscape garden and the early Picturesque garden, the art of landscape design will become stimulating and creative instead of sentimental and sterile.

There are, therefore, three methods of renewing our creative forces, which can now be summarized as follows:

1. THE FUNCTIONAL APPROACH.—Æsthetic values lie in the simple statement, in economy of the means of expression, and in discarding " the old clothes of a past age," which are the Styles. Use determines form. Garden and landscape must be humanized in accordance with the needs of the twentieth century; they can be made pleasant to live in as well as to look at. The sociological conception demands that garden and landscape become one organization, the free landscape commencing where we need it most—at the walls of the habitation.

2. THE EMPATHIC APPROACH.—Nature is not to be regarded as a refuge from life, but as an invigorator of it and a stimulus to body and mind. Nature is therefore not to be copied or sentimentalized, neither is she to be overridden. The banishment of the antagonistic, masterful attitude towards Nature, of excessive symmetry, a recognition of the value of tactile qualities in plant material, a grasp of rhythm and accent, contribute to the supple and fluid adaptation of the site, which is the landscape architect's chief arbiter of design.

3. THE ARTISTIC APPROACH.—The profitless search for decorative beauty, a purely relative quality, is abandoned in the creation of the work of art. An appreciation of the interrelation of all true forms of art and of artists themselves results in a broadening of the power of expression and in the co-operation needed for the remaking of the garden scene. Decoration and ornament, schemes of colour and pattern, must cease to occupy their present narrow niche and become

* From a manifesto issued by the Association Internationale des Architectes de Jardins Modernistes.

integral factors in the plan. Outworn systems of æsthetics and formulas of design will then make way for the experimental technique, resulting in new forms which are expressive of our own time and of ourselves.

IV— *The Planter's Eye*

1. COLOUR AND FORM

One important technical aspect of landscape planning remains to be discussed. It is not the purpose of this book to detail methods or materials, but to pencil a rough design for the modern garden and its projection into the landscape; nevertheless, in order to bring into the argument an important factual tendency it will be necessary to make some mention of planting, without perhaps altering the general character of these pages by giving many specific examples of the art. What wood, brick and stone are to the architect, plant forms are to the landscape planner; their place is not in print, but in the sketch-book— too personal a thing to be subjected to analysis in theoretical terms. To plant well is not to formulate a technique in the meaning of design or to base planting activity on textbook instruction, but to evolve a tradition of experiment which will stand superior to the traditions of past ages, elaborated for times other than our own.

It is, of course, possible to put forward æsthetic theories which will hold good for the planter's art, as well as for related activities. The author once took the trouble to collect material for such a theory, but contact with philosophers like Hegel and Lipps, though suitably edifying in the one case and illuminating in the other, could not shake his belief that æsthetic harmony cannot be felt and analysed simultaneously. Take away the body from the mind, and the latter will wither and die. In other words, the planning and making of gardens is always a more complex thing than any theory that can be held about these processes, and although there is an essential usefulness in theory as a foundation for a consistent æsthetic attitude, the landscape designer's theory, without loss of flexibility, can almost be reduced to the dimensions of a Golden Rule, and in such a form can be used by the planter to demonstrate the principles of harmony, balance and rhythm where and when he will, without looming so large as to block out his intuitive horizon.

That horizon has, in the past, been clouded by many queer confusions. In gardens, since the eighteenth century, planting has not been considered so much an organized reasoned process as a medium for the indulgence of the wildest, irrational caprice. In the landscape it has been used as an excuse for reincarnating the façade-conscious avenue designer and the nineteenth-century bourgeois planner of domestic surroundings. In each milieu the art, though ubiquitous, is at its lowest ebb, and until it can become selective instead of merely

107

liberal, and ordered rather than regimented and confined, there is little hope that the twentieth century can evolve a scene in any way comparable to that of the eighteen and early nineteen hundreds.

There are many reasons for identifying the rise and dominance of colour problems with the absence of a reliable contemporary tradition of planting, and the chief of these is one which will now be put forward. It is simply the fact that when gardeners followed the Impressionists by allowing the existence of a natural colour system rather than the selection in the studio of conventionalized tones, they failed to recognize the Impressionists' chief discovery that the earth was lit from the sky; in other words, that light was the main factor and the key to the whole situation.

The transition in painting had been gradual. The Pre-Impressionists, those of the schools of Delacroix and David, were aware that colour changed from moment to moment, but could not reconcile this phenomenon with their preconceived colour formulas learned in the academies. The school of 1830, which is typified by Corot, knew of the power of light, but chose to paint suffused rather than illuminated scenes. After them came Monet, who struck into the brightness of midday and painted the landscape of the Ile de France flooded in golden sunlight. This did not make work easy for Monet, who died at an advanced age still struggling to capture on his canvas all in that landscape that was colour, form and light, but his achievements taught others that the struggle was worth while. It is interesting to compare his long life with that of Gertrude Jekyll, the most outstanding planter since the eighteenth century, whose own covered the same period in time. Both had an almost primitive love of the soil, a passion for gathering from Nature the nourishment to sustain burning convictions and long-cherished beliefs. Both preferred an existence withdrawn from civilization, surrounded by familiar, daily-renewed contacts with the lesser inanimate things. Both suffered from failing eyesight, and both achieved greatness through work and love of the tools and methods they employed. But apart from these similarities there was a fundamental difference in their achievements. Monet, in his later years, planned and made an inspired garden, a painter's garden indeed, but an achievement acknowledged to be equal to some of his work on canvas. Jekyll, the amateur artist, on the other hand, though accomplished enough as a technician, was not of the calibre of Gertrude Jekyll, the planter. If she had been able to express herself as well with the brush as with the planter's hand, the problem of light and colour which she constantly disregarded might have been recognized and solved. As it was, in upsetting the crude Victorian

108

paintpot, she failed to provide an alternative large enough to serve as a source of inspiration for posterity.

What Gertrude Jekyll did accomplish was a careful and accurate estimate of colour effects through observation and experiment. Hers was not the eye to overlook gradations of tone in plant foliage, for instance, or the intensification of tonal value in flowers of pure colours when placed in close proximity to white.* Before her time, too, crimson might establish itself anywhere in the wide gulf between scarlet and magenta, and cerise be known as amaranthine red; systematic colour classification, though not directly of her instigation, derives from her efforts to value each shade and suggest its merited place in the garden scheme.

Such physiological colour considerations have made responsible garden planning a more accurate and scientific affair than it was in the days before tonal values were discovered as a new plaything for the academically minded designer of ribbon borders and herbaceous walks. But these tonal values in themselves have never been able to carry us very far, and in some ways it is a matter for regret that they were ever discovered at all. As Amedée Ozenfant has pointed out, since we evolved a colour science we have been afraid to employ it in a straightforward English way. If it were not for the charts of the interior decorator and the dressmaker, our favourite colours would still be the bright red and blue of the national flag, egg yellow, the tobacco brown which with white and emerald green still decorates our pleasure boats, the burnt sienna of the sails of fishing smacks and the vermilion of the pillar box. A primitive taste, perhaps, but in keeping with the English tradition. It is still strong in country and seaside places— one finds it in shop fronts, marine gardens and the black and white paintwork of Georgian architecture—but in the fashionable urban districts and polite suburbs there is a tendency towards a more subdued range and a gradual ousting of the Paul Crampel geranium from the window box. The fear of pure structural colour in gardens is leading to the practice of a muddled pointillism (a general dotting and smearing of colours), a technique which accords very well with fashion's matching and blending, but makes a strange qualification for garden artists in the country of all Europe in which the colour garden is still the only favoured style.

This queer perversion of art more than corroborates the author's own opinion that the colour garden *per se* is valueless as a contribution either to æsthetics or to the English scene. As Adrian Stokes observes in his *Colour and Form*: " Systems of colour harmonies are interesting,

* An Aristotelian conception.

but no more so than common chords played upon the piano. . . .
Colours in themselves, since they are different wave-lengths, different
parts of light, do cause definite physiological reactions; but, isolated
from form, sensation of colour does not lead to a pure art of colours, or
anything that can be called an art." The value of contrasts in colour
and even of blends lies not so much in the contrast or the blend as a
whole, but in the significance brought out in the individual tones by
juxtaposition.

It would therefore seem that the one step towards the solution of
problems of colour out of doors will be made by employment of an
empathic approach rather than by concentration on purely intellectual
variations which rely to only a small degree on emotive effect. Such
a method would at once remove the necessity for consideration of
colour planning as an end in itself—the contemporary tendency—and
substitute an ideal for colour in which this factor could play a functional part in garden planning.

But structural colour, which rests easily enough in the gloom of
Byzantine churches and the smouldering fire of Venetian painting, is
a complicated problem out of doors. A garden scene is not viewed
as a picture in a frame with neutral background and regulated lighting.
There are distractions. To weave the thread of colour pattern through
the material of a garden plan so that it strengthens and enlivens it is
necessary to provide certain conditions which will set colour free in
order to allow it to play a satisfactory part.

2. STRUCTURE AND ILLUMINATION

There is a fallacious opinion held of the quality of the English
landscape which might have been corrected in the nineteenth century
had colour planning been considered as it deserved. This is the idea
that the countryside is a soft and limpid harmony of tones and shades.
In fact, England is only querulously green, spasmodically pleasant,
and remains in general æsthetic character peculiarly complicated.
It is a country of varied but not balancing tones. The following
remarks indicate the root of the trouble:*

"In England the bright lifting colour of the ground where grass
covers it is a troublous quality. A dark hedge rises from the grass
with little vital connection. Whereas in Italy, in whose bright landscape there is a prevalence of neutral colours that gain from each
other, the earth is seen as mother and founder of the strong virile
vegetation. Evergreens radiate their warmth with a luminous dark-

* *Colour and Form*, Adrian Stokes. Faber and Faber, 1938.

ness. At night they seem to be black because they harbour the warmth and brightness of the day; it is from this dark warm store of colour that sun and sky will again take out their blue and yellow."

The increased strength of colour harmonies against warm or luminous backgrounds is a widespread but generally unnoticed phenomenon.

Green, according to Goethe, is not an emancipated flowing colour, but one which can be defined. Therefore, although it is emotionally restful and of easy focus, it is not an ideal colour for a landscape background, because the eye is always seeking opportunities to limit its spread and define a boundary. It is the warm luminous colours which cannot be contained—the tones of a dusky Mediterranean landscape and other similar littorals—which glow with an inner reflected light. In England the light presses from above. It is not the clear white light of warmer countries, but it is dominant; there is a glitter at midday on glabrous leaves and lustrous glimmering flowers which drains the life from colour so that only under a leaden sky or at twilight can a planned effect achieve its fullest value. This is an argument for the use of mass plantings of one tone or of such combinations as will be as effective in brilliant as well as subdued illumination. There is no doubt, however, that colour gradations in borders and walks often fail of their effect for the reasons given above—namely, the devitalizing power of illumination and the limiting influence of green. Extreme perspective mitigates the latter drawback to some extent, but such a device is not often possible and frequently undesirable for other reasons. So, too, does the use of flowers which hide their foliage or those which have leaves and stems of darker tones,* but these unfortunately are not the general run.

Elimination of the light overplus is impossible; therefore, it is a factor which should be acknowledged. Elimination of incompatible greens is possible in some degree, so that colour can be liberated to perform its work. In practice the two factors can be controlled in landscape planting—in the one case by an emphasis on form, and in the other by the use of chiaroscuro and plant illuminants.

The problem of form in planting has for so long received less attention than that of colour that the two qualities have been estranged and the former become a question merely of outline and silhouette.

---

* The mid-green leaf tone is one which is balanced best by certain shades of purple and orange, but generally speaking it is more unfortunate than the rarer yellow-greens and blue-greens (usually chosen by the painters), which absorb light and are sustained by it, and can therefore be set against a much larger scale of colour values.

A textural garden for an open-air restaurant by a Swiss designer. Purely decorative colour plays only an incidental part in the scheme of planting.

As we have seen, it is a misfortune to consider colour as an end in itself; it is equally unfortunate that formal problems, when considered at all, have been isolated in a similar arbitrary fashion. It is not sufficient for the purposes of landscape design to classify plants as " weeping," " prostrate," " globose," " columnar," or " pyramidal," without reference to effects of light and shade and depth and variation of colour tones, which may accentuate or nullify the formal composition. It is not likely, for instance, that the most strikingly formal of all hardy trees, the Chilean pine, would have the same significance in outline or in mass were its foliage pale green rather than the strong hard *terre verte* to which we are accustomed. The relation between form and colour is so close that the first quality cannot exist without the other. Although the mind has come to separate colour and form, the eye cannot; colour, after all, is the appreciable result of a process of light reflection, and we can only visualize the form of plants by the quality and quantity of the light reflected from them. Even the forms we see in half-lights are bound by colour, for in darkness hover all the light reflections which are stored within the mind. The eighteenth-century landscape gardeners knew something of this;* further, they may have been aware that concentration on problems of colour would not improve their art. In any case, they decided that landscapes were to remain studies in green forms,† and banished the flower garden to hidden places behind walls and hedges.

* Pope, and through him Southcote and Spence, were among those who recognized the variable worth of green forms in landscape composition.

† Today certain Swiss and Scandinavian designers follow the same rule in concentrating increasingly on textural rather than colour effects in planting.

112

No doubt they discovered that colour arbitrarily introduced was apt to draw the eye from the structural tones of the landscape artificially composed in itself, yet balanced by reason of its formal bias. All colour values in landscape must be translated by their relationship with backgrounds; therefore, it was better not to make comparisons with green, except in the sense that form means outline, as we have considered. They knew that colour and form are structurally and pictorially inseparable.

Inseparable, but mutually destructive in the landscape, for, although forms and colours can balance each other, in Nature they often fail to do so. Take, for example, the nebulous shape of a yew tree on the chalk downs, where it appears sporadically and grows to greater perfection than many other evergreens. Against the rolling light green grassland it has no connection, no vital link of similarity or even of contrast to weld it to the surrounds. The grass lifts up, the yew tree weighs it down; there is a lack of balance in colours and in forms. See the same tree against the jagged whiteness of a chalk-pit, and the æsthetic effect is at once satisfactory. The dark shape looms strongly against a contrasting background, which welcomes it because the contrast is in kind. The intensity of tone in tree and soil is similar, and therefore mutually enhancing; they draw together, yet individually gain a larger character. Similarly, a yew tree on a lawn is less powerful emotively than one placed in relationship to buildings; from the grey stones of a churchyard it draws the illumination necessary to enhance its form. So, too, in gardens, the isolated phenomenon of

a previously mentioned example, the Chilean pine, architectural in outline, unless grown in an open landscape in sufficient numbers, needs architectural treatment to be seen to best advantage. Place it alone among the tender greens of deciduous foliage, and its character is drawn from it; but grown in a white-walled courtyard away from other trees, it takes on the precision of a machine. Such a

A green corner in a garden by Otto Valentien of Stuttgart.

situation can support the use of structural colour. The author brings to mind a well-grown *Araucaria imbricata* within the angle of two such walls and towering above them; beyond the spread of its branches in summer lie flat rectangles of scarlet geraniums arranged in a simple pattern. The courtyard is paved with neutral coloured stone. The intensity of tone decreases through the white, scarlet and dark green of the three principal colours, but in progression, for red is the after-image of white and green of red.* A balance is thus held between the forms and each gains from the other. The red tide at the base of the tree surges forwards and upwards through the dark stem as though to bring it an increased life and strength.

The foregoing is an example of the structural power of colour as distinct from · its pictorial qualities. Naturally we should demand wider use of structural colour than that indicated by such a simple instance. For although structural colour is always strong and vibrant, it can also be delicate and subtle by transposition to another key. Such delicacy is often called for where colour is employed to illuminate intricate growing forms; in fact, if it were wise to formulate any definite colour rules, one of the first would be that intensity of tone may diminish in direct proportion to the growth in complexity of forms. There is a sound practical reason for this remark in the fact that light reflection is normally increased by complication of plane surfaces— a condition which tends to lessen the intensity of colour. Surface colours of the forms employed will also tend to modify such arrangements, which in the last resort depend for effectiveness on local factors which cannot always be foreseen.

To build with colour away from architectural surroundings which tend to provide the neutral background of the picture gallery or the warm tones of a more favourable landscape, invites the creation in the open garden or landscape of conditions in which colour can exist. It has been said that an emphasis of formal values will be necessary under these open conditions, and where outline is emphasized colour may very well play a minor part.† So things perhaps will be when the modern eye is trained to appreciate colour in its proper place. But to banish colour from the designed landscape would be too arbitrary a proceeding altogether. As we have seen, it is a factor which may be helpful physiologically to the appreciation of form, and further, in mass it can be used to balance defined and also coloured formal arrangements.

* Scientific evidence exists to support this statement (Ostwald).
† The illustration on page 113 shows a green composition which has no need of additional colour to emphasize its formal arrangement.

114

A method of setting colour free, in these circumstances, is provided by the use of background plants which cannot be defined as we have seen that green can be defined—*i.e.*, illuminants which tend to spread and absorb the light and their surroundings. In everyday planters' material such tones are readily found in the yellow and silver foliage of certain variegated evergreen and deciduous shrubs, in the vinous purple and bronze red of many Chinese and American trees and shrubs, and in the opaque darkness of familiar evergreens like holly and yew. Certain grey-greens and, again, the yellow-greens may be compatible also with structural colour effects; in fact, it is better not to limit but to suggest, since among the enormous range of contemporary plant material gradations of foliage colour will always be found to supply the needs of transition from one colour harmony to another. It is possible, therefore, by grading the planted background, to arrange that any suitable tone shall stand out in a place where structural colour is required; against that tone pure colour effects may be obtained (usually and preferably through the use of plants which either hide their foliage with blossom or bear a foliage character other than green) which become a part of that background, and therefore have a reason for their existence. The physiological colour-stimulus of any such arrangements is thus allowed full play and achieves a greater value as a component of the composition's theme.

It is not suggested that this method of planting should involve a preponderance of variegated-leaved plants, of sombre evergreens, and generally of plants with a leaf tint other than the definable greens; all that it implies is the simple but generally unrecognized fact that in introducing massed colour effects out of doors for physiological or emotional stimulation it is necessary to bring colour also into the backgrounds which help to create these effects. In its present state, colour in landscape planning is applied in purely decorative and non-structural fashion against ill-considered backgrounds which frequently have not been chosen with an eye to the general purpose in view. It is time, therefore, that some attempt similar to the method given, which is admittedly only a small and imperfect beginning, should be made to give colour its proper place in the varied pattern of the out-of-door scene.

If these observations on the formal qualities of colour can be related in a practical fashion to landscape planning without allowing them too arbitrary an importance, the position may be stated as follows:

1. The green landscapes of England demand a formal emphasis—*i.e.*, their æsthetic appreciation can safely be allowed to remain an

115

appreciation of outline, contours and drawn lines, coupled with a visual emphasis of tones rather than of hues.

2. Colour can under certain conditions revivify these tones and renew the structural life of landscape (*a*) through concentration of purely physiological colour in architectural surroundings which nourish it and lessen the devitalizing power of light in a heavy northern atmosphere, (*b*) through employment of the methods of chiaroscuro (light coming out of darkness) or of illuminative backgrounds in the open garden or larger landscape compositions.

The problems of colour and form in mass planting are but a fraction of the planter's cares. Indeed, one reason for emphasizing them has been to corroborate the axiom earlier put forward concerning Nature and Art—*i.e.*, that it is wrong to suggest that Nature is always pleasing, and therefore a garden composed of natural growing things must necessarily be æsthetically satisfying.* A garden as a work of art is only natural in relation to its materials; it is a product of the imagination (a faculty, certainly dependent on Nature for nourishment, but free to dream in bold unearthly ways), and as such is the artist's expression of himself. It follows that trees, flowers and stones in the garden are in a sense artificial objects, and are valuable only in relation to their surroundings or to the feelings they arouse in the beholder. In the words of Aristotle, " a landscape is a state of the soul." Why is the rhythmical, upward movement in the branches of a sombre fir so warming to the heart, so expressive of our own struggle towards the heights of human experience? Why do we remain unmoved by the sight of a thicket of silver birches (provided that silver birches are a commonplace in our lives), while a group of these graceful trees trembling in the wind on the crest of a grassy mound can move us to exclamations of delight?

We only know that we are apt to read our own feelings of ease or difficulty of progression into natural forms, and our sensations of variety and monotony into the character of their shapes. Our bodily attitudes of rising or falling, standing or lying, as well as our sensibilities, also influence our reactions to the parts of a landscape which possess these characteristics. We know, too, that we are apt to pass over scenes in Nature which displease us and linger where the harmony of a framework of trees or a balancing cloud can give us satisfaction. As Shenstone said, " The eye must be easy before it can be pleased."

So it is that (without neglect of the charm and value of the adventitious plant) relationships must be studied in planting, just as in

---

* Mill's precept *Naturam observare*, rather than the doctrine *Naturam sequii*, applies equally to Art as to other human activities.

painting, music, town planning or any other form of composition. To appreciate formal relationships, whether they be of texture and outline as modern Scandinavian and Swiss designers find them, or of mood and feeling as developed by the eighteenth-century Romantics in the grotto and the wilderness, must be part of the education of the landscape designer. And the life that breathes in inanimate things—in the patterns of a pebble-strewn path or a carpet of pine needles—must voice itself to him as strongly as the miracle of growth. The rich fulfilment of the promise of its foliage by the acanthus flower* need be no less gratifying to observe than the shadow of a summer cloud racing over the lawn. What the tree gains from the soil is life, yet the soil lives too within the artist's mind, which gathers and renews all significant material in Nature. To plant is but a part of landscape composition; to co-ordinate is all.

* The æsthetic appreciation of plant forms is older in origin than the appreciation of the arrangement of these forms. "... A patch of dark blue rue paints the shady grove; it has short leaves and throws out short umbels, and passes the breath of the wind and the rays of the sun right down to the end of the stalk, and at a gentle touch gives forth a heavy scent."—*Wahlafrid Strabo, circa* 827-840.

ARCHITECTS' PLANTS

The plants illustrated are intended as examples of useful structural material and have not been chosen especially for their interest when in flower. Nor are they strictly the *formes architecturales* which M. Correvon, the Swiss plantsman, has taken pains to identify, but are rather a selection from those subjects which in various ways can be employed to contribute to the shape or atmosphere of certain familiar settings. The cultural details apply only to Great Britain. The sketches are by Gordon Cullen.

Hardy Plants for an Exotic Effect

Yucca gloriosa (Adam's Needle), Phormium tenax (New Zealand Flax) Dracœna australis (Cordyline), Trachycarpus Fortunei (Chusan Palm). These plants are suitable for courtyards, the angles of terrace walls and similar places which are not exposed to north or east winds. They are hardy at Kew in sheltered situations and will grow on most soils, but prefer light, well-drained ones, and withstand drought well. All are excellent for sunny seaside gardens, but with the exception of the yucca are not recommended for planting north of the Thames. In very favoured situations the American agave can be added to this list. The New Zealand flax has been sketched with its seed containers hanging empty. Be-

fore they reach this stage the flower stems are excellent for interior decoration. The yucca is the most commonly grown of the plants illustrated and has done duty on many a rock garden where "something striking" has been considered necessary to offset the monotony of large stretches of close-growing plants and stones. It shows to greater advantage in an architectural setting—on a roof garden or on the terrace. Winter damp and snow does it more harm than frost. The veronica in the foreground is an unidentified species which happened to be in the artist's path.

Room Plants

Tradescantia zebrina (Wandering Jew); P. tobira (Pittosporum); Aralia veitchii;
Dracæna sanderiana; Philodendron cordatum; Euonymus var. silver queen.
Plants which are required to stand indoors for some time (very few can perman-
ently withstand atmospheric conditions which human beings find agreeable) are
best kept in the original pots in which they are supplied by the nurseryman, and
plunged in a container such as the one shown, which is lined with zinc and filled
with peat or sphagnum fibre. This helps to prevent the roots from drying out;
consequently, frequent use of the water-can, which in inexperienced hands is a
source of danger to most room plants, can be dispensed with. Spraying the foliage
with a fine syringe, however, cannot be done too often, and another advantage of
the peat bed is that it tends to absorb the consequent drip from the leaves. None
of the plants illustrated is showy in flower, since flowering plants indoors need
very frequent renewal. The creeping Tradescantia zebrina (used here as ground
cover) does provide some colour when in bloom, but its chief interest lies in the
leaves, which are striped on the upper surface and rose red underneath. The stems
are attenuated and straying, from which comes the plant's common name of
Wandering Jew. The plant with the slender stem and digitate leaflets is Aralia
veitchii, while the contrasting foliage next to it belongs to the familiar Rubber
Plant. The striped grass-like subject below is Dracæna sanderiana, which comes
from the Congo and lasts well under trying conditions. The climber trailing across
the picture is Philodendron cordatum. Its smooth, leathery leaves are easily
syringed clean. The variegated evergreen shrub, against the pillar, Euonymus var.
silver queen has already been mentioned, but not illustrated in this series. The
Pittosporum tobira next to it is a near-hardy shrub which lasts well indoors and
does not seem to be subject to scale or other insect pests. The plants sketched are
actually growing in the staircase-well of a block of flats, where they receive little
direct daylight. A much wider range of subjects can be chosen for the plant window.

Variegated Evergreens

Vinca major elegantissima (golden periwinkle); Elæagnus pungens aureo-variegata (golden oleaster). This is a class of shrubs valuable in winter, when their leaves make a cheerful garden decoration, and towards the end of the summer, after the majority of shrubs have finished flowering. Varieties should be chosen with care, however; only those with bright, well-defined variegation are really effective out-of-doors. This characteristic is possessed by the two examples shown, and the golden periwinkle, known by nurserymen as Vinca major elegantissima, has the additional advantage of producing porcelain blue flowers from May to December. This is the small trailing subject drawn to a larger scale on the right of the sketch. Next to it is Elæagnus pungens aureo-variegata, which also has golden variegation, arranged in broad irregular bands down the centre of the leaf, and is probably the most highly coloured of all. Its growth is thick and spreading. For those who prefer white or cream-coloured variegation, the creeping Euonymus radicans variegata and the upright-growing variety Silver Queen are useful and attractive.

These and the periwinkle will grow under the drip of trees. The twiggy deciduous shrub in the background of the sketch is Viburnum fragrans, not long introduced from North China. It makes a pleasant foil to the evergreens, is perfectly hardy, and is valuable in blooming from October until early April. Its whitish flowers have a heliotrope scent, which on warm winter days carries for many yards. The inset illustration shows a detail of the flower. All the plants mentioned are accommodating as to soil and position.

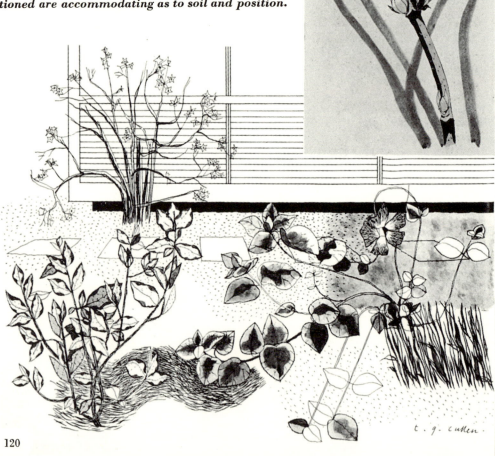

Conifers

Juniperus chinensis Pfitzeriana (spreading Chinese Juniper); Araucaria imbricata (Chilean Pine); Picea excelsa pendula (weeping European Spruce). The cone-bearing trees as a whole are useful in gardens for their varying evergreen shapes; among this large class only very few kinds are deciduous. The sketch shows three types of conifer having contrasting habits of growth—semi-prostrate, regular pyramidal and contorted weeping forms. In the foreground of the sketch (on the steps of the terrace) are shown two young specimens of the spreading Chinese Juniper, one of many semi-prostrate conifers, of which the savins are the best-known examples. This one has horizontal branches with pendulous tips and is grey-green in colour. It does not object to a dry soil. The familiar Monkey Puzzle or Chilean Pine (shown to the right) is best given a position by itself or grouped with its own kind—young plants on a lawn make a dark star-like pattern which is some-times a pleasant change from the less precise growth of many other trees. As they get older the plants often lose their lower branches, unless they are in a very sheltered position. This specimen was sketched at Kew, where the atmospheric conditions are unfavourable. They grow to perfection in the warmer, moister parts of the country, where they sometimes produce their edible seeds. A detail appears on the extreme right. The weeping European Spruce, seen beyond on the left, is a curiosity of variable form. Its main stem, draped with short pendulous branches, usually develops one or more sinuous bends, which give the tree an apparently unstable character. In landscape planting this convulsive habit of growth introduces an arresting quality of movement. It grows best in a medium, moist loam.

H

121

Plants with grey foliage

Romneya trichocalyx (Matilija Poppy); *Hosta Fortunei* (Plantain Lily); *Allium* species and varieties (Ornamental Onions). *Plants with grey foliage and yellow flowers are not difficult to find; sometimes, however, grey and white make a more effective combination for the garden. Here are three suggestions for plants with whitish inflorescences which will be found useful architecturally, for example to link concrete walls and ramps about the house, as in the sketch. Romneya trichocalyx, on the right beyond the ramp, belongs to the poppy family. It comes from California, and is not hardy enough in most places here to plant very far from a sunny protecting wall. Even then it is better to cut the old growth down to the ground each spring; new stems will grow six to eight feet in a season and flower profusely in June, as well as intermittently thereafter throughout the season. It prefers a well-drained stony soil. The special requirements of the Matilija Poppy are more than compensated for by the architectural character of its stems, foliage and flowers. No plant could be more desirable for a favoured place near the terrace. Care should be taken to plant R. trichocalyx and not R. Coulteri, which is more commonly known, but flowers less freely in our climate. By the water's edge is shown Hosta Fortunei, one of the Plantain Lilies, a herbaceous plant with blue-grey foliage and lilac-white flowers. Members of the genus Hosta, or Funkia, as it is sometimes called, like a deep, moist soil in which to develop their deeply ribbed root leaves. The clumps improve with age and may be left undisturbed for many years. Some ornamental members of the onion family appear on the left of the sketch. Allium ampeloprasum leucanthum with its globular heads of flowers is nearest the stone wall; to its right is the so-called Welsh Onion, which comes from Siberia. The latter has no distinct bulb, but the variety shown produces aerial onions among the leaves, a surprising conceit which accounts in part for its presence in the picture. As semi-permanent glaucous subjects the onions have distinct garden value.*

Woody Plants
for Sandy Soil

Genista Ætnensis (The Etna Broom); Tamarix pentandra (Tamarisk). The two subjects illustrated are useful for planting on sandy banks and borders where close screens are not required, although the Tamarisk (on right of sketch) can be trained to make a hedge by the sea-side if cut back each April. Its showy pink flowers are produced in July and August, when comparatively few shrubs are in bloom. This species is preferable to the spring-flowering kinds, which need cutting back after flowering, and care should be taken to obtain T. pentandra (or T. hispida œstivalis, as it is sometimes called). The Etna Broom (left) needs very little pruning, and should be allowed to obtain its full height of twenty to thirty feet, after shortening the growth during the first two years to induce bushiness. The bark of its elegant, slightly pendulous branches becomes yellow with age and the whole shrub is conspicuous for its almost complete absence of leaves. It, too, flowers in summer, rather later than most brooms. There is much to commend in its habit of growth. The twisted branches and the delicate, whip-like younger shoots make a perfect response to any unbroken architectural surface.

Gordon Cullen.

Shrubs for the Roof Garden

Ligustrum coriaceum (Japanese Privet); Cytisus albus (White Spanish Broom);
Genista hispanica (Spanish Gorse). Although there are many lesser plants which
will thrive on roof gardens, the majority of shrubs do not like the usual dry con-
ditions and restricted root room of the average soil container in such situations.
Those illustrated are three which will grow in about fifteen inches of soil in exposed
positions, if adequate drainage and a good compost are provided. The stiffly erect

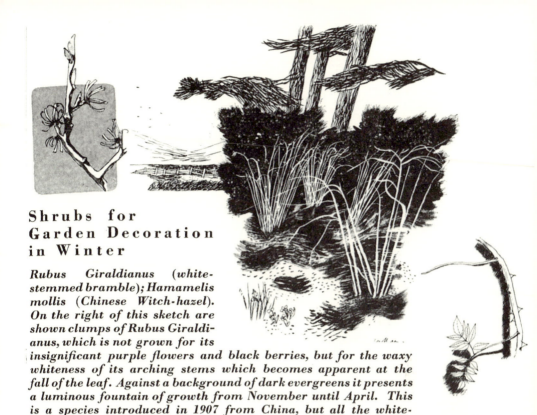

Shrubs for Garden Decoration in Winter

Rubus Giraldianus (white-stemmed bramble); Hamamelis mollis (Chinese Witch-hazel). On the right of this sketch are shown clumps of Rubus Giraldianus, which is not grown for its insignificant purple flowers and black berries, but for the waxy whiteness of its arching stems which becomes apparent at the fall of the leaf. Against a background of dark evergreens it presents a luminous fountain of growth from November until April. This is a species introduced in 1907 from China, but all the white-stemmed brambles are effective and accommodating. The stoutness and waxiness of their stems, however, is improved by planting in a rich loam. A good loam, with the addition of some leaf mould in the early stages of growth, is also the best medium for the slow-growing Chinese Witch-hazel seen on the left. This bears fragrant, yellow flowers in bunches on the bare twigs very early in the year. The curious petals are strap-shaped and elegantly waved but not crimped like those of the Japanese Witch-hazel. There is a newish variety of the latter called H. japonica flavopurpurascens, the petals of which are stained with crimson. These showy Asiatic kinds have eclipsed the smaller-flowered Virginian Witch-hazel in gardens, but the latter is still well worth growing for its subtle perfume. It owes its popular name, not to the supposed efficacy of the decoctions made from the bark and leaves, but to the use of the twigs by early American settlers for dowsing.*

---

shrub in the background of the sketch (and inset) is a stunted garden form of the Japanese Privet discovered by Robert Fortune. It has thick leathery leaves and is hardier than some of the Oriental Privets, the plant illustrated having withstood at least one cold winter in its present position. It stands in rugged contrast to the next plant, which is the White Spanish Broom, whose whip-like growth will spread for many feet. This plant is the only really hardy broom with white flowers, and its roots do not rob those of other plants . . . a point to be considered, when small containers are used. A stake is necessary for the main stem in the early stages of growth. The close-growing spiny plant in the foreground is the yellow-flowered Spanish Gorse, which forms spreading dark green hummocks in the minimum of soil and under dry conditions. It flowers profusely in early summer if given a position in full sun.*

GARDEN INTO LANDSCAPE

I.—Gardens in the Modern Landscape

LANDSCAPE into garden. . . . This fusion took place in the eighteenth century. As we have seen, social and economic forces contributed to the metamorphosis; Italian painters, English poets and Chinese craftsmen influenced its form. Perhaps nothing less than a social and economic revolution will enable men to garden landscapes once again, but a predetermination of the form of the new landscape will be the first logical step towards its realization.

The new landscape is the garden without boundaries.

Garden into landscape. . . .

The garden has always been subject to two main influences—the outer influence from the landscape and the inner from the house. These are fluctuating primary influences, only one of which we are at present in a position to control.

Interpreting these influences in terms applicable to the garden is another matter. But if we believe, as perhaps can be concluded from the previous section of this book, that inspiration can be drawn from the underlying principles of contemporary life and art, then the problem becomes capable of solution.

For the garden of today cannot be called contemporary in spirit, as can the modern movements in architecture, sculpture or painting. It is not of our time, but of the sentimental past; a body with no head and very little heart. Imagination is dead, romance a mere excuse for extravagance in decoration. Contemporary garden design has not even yet caught up with contemporary trends in architecture. It is to be hoped that in the near future garden-makers will become aware of this fact, and that instead of re-hashing old styles to fit new buildings they will create something more expressive of the contemporary spirit and something more worthy of the tradition to which they are the heirs.

The great white bird of modern architecture has therefore not yet found a secure and decorative perch such as would be provided in a truly modern setting. When the new materials find their way into the surroundings of our habitations, when concrete ramps, glass screens and steel pergolas become more common, those critics who consider modern architecture a purely urban style may decide to alter their opinions. If they are fearful of the incongruity of the new materials

126

in their eighteenth-century landscapes, let them be comforted by the knowledge that it will not be long before new and more fitting landscapes will be created. Within a few decades the need for new backgrounds will become imperative, and the urban landscape for the urban style is not beyond the bounds of possibility. When the idea of the garden city has been shelved and the *ville contemporaine* become a reality it will be possible to plan the country-side for enjoyment once again. Yet until they are completely changed, those eighteenth-century landscapes which remain will suffice for most of us and can be adapted for our needs. There are few honest people who would say, for instance, that the house in the landscape illustrated on page 129 is not at home in its surroundings—the work of mid-eighteenth-century planters.

In Thomas Sharp's book, *Town and Countryside*, the factors which make for harmony between house and landscape are analysed as follows:

" The assimilation of a building into the natural scene depends on two things: on the congruity (or harmony or unity) of its artificial materials, and in the form or silhouette of the buildings with the general form of the surrounding landscape." Discussing the first factor, Mr. Sharp arrives at the conclusion that where materials of a sympathetic colouring and texture are no longer obtainable " it is advisable to cover inharmonious materials in wall surfaces with a warm soft-toned colour wash." In this he includes tones approximating to white and cites as an æsthetically satisfying example the homogeneous whitewashed tenants' houses on Lord Barnard's great estate in Southwest Durham. One wonders if those critics of some modern architecture who complain of its unnaturally light colouring have ever looked at Regency buildings or visited parts of these islands beyond the south of England and East Anglia. What will their reaction be to the sight of the first glass village ? They fail, of course, to realize that the architect has now left the period of self-effacement which resulted in the wholly naturalistic style now happily departing, and is secure in his new architectural faith of bold and fitting construction.

A vindication of the new attitude occurs in Aldous Huxley's novel *Chrome Yellow*, published in 1921, in which he says :

" The house of an intelligent, civilized and sophisticated man should never seem to have sprouted from the clods. It should rather be an expression of his grand unnatural remoteness from the cloddish life. Since the days of William Morris that is a fact which we in England have been unable to comprehend. Civilized and sophisticated men have solemnly played at being peasants. Hence quaintness, arts and crafts, cottage architecture and all the rest of it. In the suburbs of our cities you may see, reduplicated in endless rows, studiedly quaint imitations and adaptations of the village hovel. Poverty, ignorance, and a limited range of materials produced the hovel. . . . We now employ our wealth, our technical knowledge, our rich variety of materials for the purpose of building millions of imitation hovels in totally unsuitable surroundings. Could imbecility go further?"

On the question of silhouette, Mr. Sharp, while not apparently having the new style in mind, takes pains to point out the importance of the horizontal line in building and suggests anchorage in the form of curtain walls linking façade to boundary.

In reality, the extreme horizontal emphasis of window and floor levels and cantilevered balconies which is so often the accompaniment of the new building will call for much more than the usual so-called " formal garden " generally in evidence somewhere near the house. Terraces, hedges, borders and paving, together with newer forms like glass and metal screens and concrete walls, all following these horizontal lines, may help to provide the anchorage which ensures the stability of the house in the landscape. This may indeed come to be the chief function of the architectural garden. As a factor of arbitration in the disputes that unfortunately still arise between local authorities and progressive architects, the use of this type of garden may help to show how sympathetically the dwelling may be welded to the soil. Less obtrusively, the irregular " atmospheric " planting of the landscape garden can achieve the same effect. Individual sites must dictate which type of garden (or balance of combinations of both types) is employed, but a freer technique than that used in the past will be the most striking characteristic of the new garden. The faith of the designer in the probity of the creative act and his avoidance of the academic symbolism of the styles, the servile imitation of natural scenes, and outworn systems of æsthetics, will result in new forms significant of the age from which they spring. It has been stated as the author's belief that a study of certain manifestations of modern art and science, together with the use of a practical system of æsthetics, would make possible the evolution

128

of a fluid contemporary technique for garden planning. This, with
the help of closer co-operation between the engineer architect, landscape architect, and town planner and a general realization that landscape and garden planning are functional problems rather than ones
concerned with parasitic ornamentation, would without doubt eventually rid us of the romantic derivative apologies for garden schemes
which are in evidence today.*

We can depend upon the fact that the new materials, concrete,
steel and glass (the latter in its new forms), will find their way into
landscape whether we wish them there or not; science and economic

* Even the best of modern planning schemes, not excepting the imaginative and
highly organized projects of le Corbusier, include garden lay-outs which are adaptations rather than pure creative works.

Above, part of the architectural garden at St. Ann's Hill. It is approached from the house through a glass-walled room devoted to the culture of tender plants. Opposite, view from the roof garden towards the swimming pool. The latter was designed to follow the curve of a clump of Rhododendron ponticum. The new work was planned and the old garden restored by the author. The architect was Raymond McGrath.

necessity are forces too strong to be denied. It is the duty of the landscape architect, as well as the architect, to adapt and use these materials in harmonious compositions. In this the gardener has today been given a lead by the architect, just as yesterday the architect was himself influenced by the ideas of that great gardener Joseph Paxton.

Behind the resentment against the new style and materials is our sentimental attachment to the past, which is a stumbling block to many forms of progress outside the sphere of art. One of the most persistent examples of this are the many societies whose aim is the preservation of the eighteenth-century landscape. It is apparent to

130

all of us that the countryside of the age-before-machines is disappearing, but what is not so clear is the necessity for the sterilization of large areas of precious and often productive land in an effort to stem the outflow from the towns. Restrictive " zoning " might be an acceptable solution to the present problem were it accompanied by sound and rational town and country planning, but sterilization as an end in itself, of which the present efforts of various societies seem to consist, cannot but lead to eventual chaos, and congestion to the point of social strangulation. We must find room for the spreading population from the towns into the countryside, but is there any reason why the move cannot be accomplished in a less short-sighted manner ?

The point that must be made here is that expansion need not mean destruction, as will inevitably happen if regulations remain as obstructive to systematized planning as they are at present. A planned England would not be an England devoid of trees, grass, flowers, blue sky and open spaces. Scientific agricultural development will not necessarily banish the lark from English meadows, and perhaps the cultivation of large planned areas may protect him from those present intrusions on his privacy which the motor-car has made almost unavoidable. Trees and plants may flourish even better than in the

hedgerow when they are systematically planted and their future development planned, as the owners of the remaining great estates can testify. Rusticity may depart in some measure, but the glory that is England's green fields, her trees and summer flowers will always remain. And are we losing much by sacrificing the character of rusticity to ordered development in the countryside? An eighteenth-century England abhorred it as heartily as we abhor a muddy and impassable road until Wordsworth and the great Romantics, frightened of what man had created in the new machines, cried out for a return to all that rural solitude implied.

All this is apparent in contrast to the new laws which can govern landscape design. Appreciation of the structure of things, of balance and controlled development, goes with an acceptance of the landscape planned for form and with imagination. We cannot all have Addison's " champain " view in this year of grace, and in the future perhaps we shall not be able to look for a hill-top without seeing some building or other astride the middle distance, though perhaps the idea of flats for country dwellers may not make this a universal necessity. We can console ourselves with the thought that the walled Cha-no-Yu garden often takes the place of a whole country of landscape to the Japanese. Without the unbroken view of our forefathers the prospect may yet be a pleasing one, and when our descendants are born into a world of planned landscape it is not likely that they will object to the appearance of buildings in country which they have never known as unencumbered. Disorder may be unpleasant to them. And after all is there not a tradition of orderliness in England? Listen to William Morris on the subject of our " little land ":

" . . . There are no great wastes overwhelming in their dreariness, no great solitudes of forest, no terrible untrodden mountain walls; all is measured, mingled, varied, gliding easily one thing into another; little rivers, little plains, swelling and speedily changing uplands, all beset with handsome orderly trees; little hills, little mountains, netted over with the walls of sheepwalks; all of it little, yet not foolish or blank, but serious rather, and abundant of meaning for such as choose to seek; it it is neither prison nor palace, but a decent home."

Our plea for order and form in garden design is of equal importance in the sphere of the countryside. We have seen how necessary is a plan for gardens—how the so-called " natural garden " is a contradiction. Cannot we have a plan for the countryside which will combine with economic sufficiency a new æsthetic heritage? It cannot be our purpose here to attempt an exposition of regional planning, which is " that new science, the projection of the whole life of the community," and is necessarily bound up with economics and social legislation. But if we can experiment with gardens and remake our immediate surroundings into areas of imagery and order, it is likely that the influence may spread into a wider sphere, and one as badly in need of imaginative control.

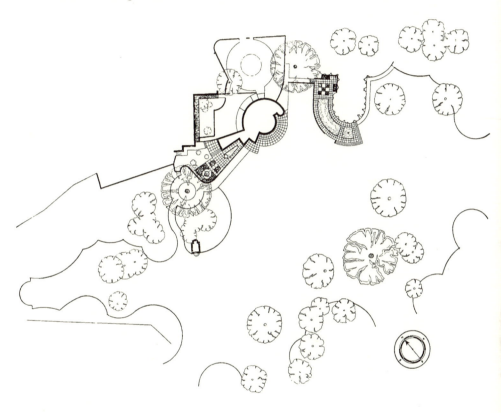

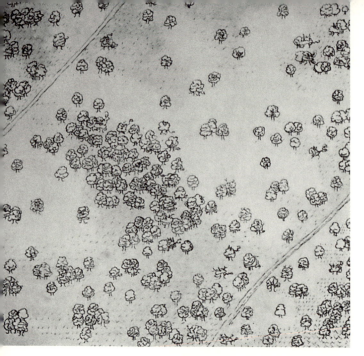

17th Century

A virgin tract of the original Windsor forest. Oak trees predominate. Primitive tracks run through open glades.

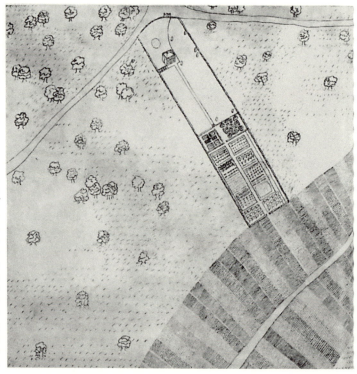

1700: Pre-Landscape

The forest cleared. The tracks become roads, along one of which the soil is cultivated in strips. A house with formal garden bounded by rectilinear walls. A simple lawn around the house; the rest of the garden geometrically planted, mostly for practical use. Even the decorative box-edged Dutch garden is planted with culinary herbs.

THE GARDEN IN THE LANDSCAPE
A SUMMARY OF CHARACTERISTIC DEVELOPMENT OVER 200 YEARS

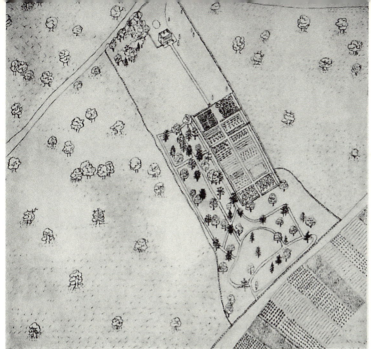

1725: Transition Period

Inclosure by land-owner; more land is taken into the garden. The cultivation disappears from one side of the road. Planting of new trees, including conifers, to form an irregular wood instead of formal avenues: the "wilderness" of Batty Langley, with winding walks.

1760: Early Landscape Period

The strip cultivation has now all disappeared, and is replaced by the typical park landscape. Informal planting of a belt of mixed trees along either road. A winding walk among them. New clumps in the landscape. Cedars on the lawn. The formal garden disappears, to make way for an uninterrupted lawn around the house, a typical innovation of Lancelot Brown. A screen of trees hides the kitchen garden. A sunk fence, or ha-ha, provides the least obtrusive garden boundary.

135

1810: Late Landscape Period

The grounds are extended to take in a small ornamental farm. The house is rebuilt in the Regency style and a conservatory added. Architectural features, a classical temple, a grotto and a tea house, are brought in to adorn the garden scene in the fashion set by Repton. The cedars have grown rapidly.

1850: Victorian Period

Victorian complication of plan. The house is enlarged and the lawn in front of the house is broken up again with flower-beds, shrubberies and paths. A range of glass-houses (this is the age of Paxton). The formal garden has returned to its own site; this time for "bedding out." Hedges supplant the ha-ha.

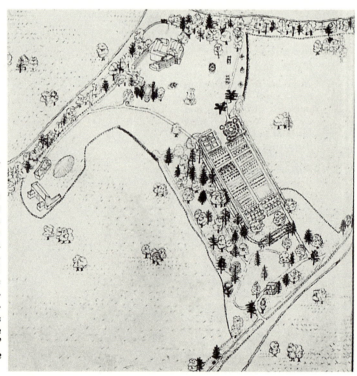

136

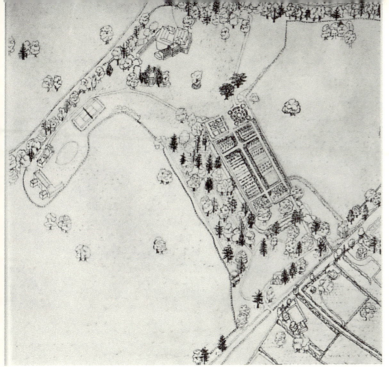

1910

The small flower-beds have been cleared away, but new twentieth-century features arrive: a tennis court; a row of villas in rectangular plots along the road. A villa on the near side of the road encroaches on the estate itself. Herbaceous borders of hardy plants make their appearance in the kitchen garden: the influence of Gertrude Jekyll. The shrubberies have become massed groups of rhododendrons.

1938

The garden as it is today, photographed from the air: St. Anne's Hill, Chertsey, a modern garden in the remains of an eighteenth-century landscape. The formal and kitchen gardens remain; also the careful planting in clumps; but unnecessary paths have been removed and the whole scene simplified. The house has been rebuilt in reinforced concrete and around it formal modern garden elements (see page 130) link the modern house to the scene, but still fit aptly in the park-like setting.

I

*In the landscape photograph above the planting in the garden
which occupies the foreground (in contrast to that in the
garden shown in the series of reconstructions on the preceding
pages) is only of thirty years' standing, and has lately been
remodelled by the author. That of the middle distance (a
" belt " on the borders of a developed estate) is about the same
age, while the wooded pastureland beyond is approximately
100 years older. The whole area lies within twenty-five miles
of London.*

II—Community Gardens

IT is time to consider the surroundings of our homes and workplaces, not as fixed units, fenced in and exclusively enjoyed, but as
part of the ordered development of the countryside. The garden
of tomorrow will not be the hedged, personal, half-acre of today, but
a unit of the broad green landscape itself, controlled for the benefit
of all.

Today the suburban plot, tomorrow the garden without limitation.
Unless this comes about, the communal dwelling will contain less of
humanity than the beehive and remain a storage place for human
beings. We have come to realize that now with the first deplorable
results of slum clearance schemes in evidence about us. But let us be
careful in our method of approach to the new problem and not let the
humanism of the gardener's philosophy depart from us. The idea
of the garden must envelop and permeate our attitude to town planning. It must supersede those barren and stereotyped notions of street
planting, classic open-air civic centres, rigid parkway systems and

138

other grandiose types of development which make present-day schemes of the so-called " garden city " school of planning such empty and cumbersome achievements.

The planning of living areas, parks, sports centres, allotments and factory surrounds must be made part of a rational garden approach. Treat them as part of the social fabric in a pattern of verdure, or they will continue to be characterless and isolated factors making for the deterioration of town and countryside.

The retention of the garden attitude in landscape planning does not, as might be inferred from this phrase, imply an especially floral or even broadly horticultural approach. The conventional garden city is consistently lacking in concentration and in clearness of design. It is the humanization of the landscape which demands the abandoning of the attitude of the typical town planner. (Civic ostentation is but a phenomenon of the individualist creed.) If the private garden is relegated to its proper place as an accessory to make room for something which will serve the community in a more fitting manner, it will be essential to discard also the " pretty-pretty " attitude of so many professional people whose business involves the consideration of plant material. Planning for amenities too often involves applied decoration in the form of planters' set-pieces. By all means let Nature be with us in and around our homes, but only on the understanding that she performs some useful function. The new garden art " must submit itself to the demands of society and fulfil with efficiency an active rôle in the physical and mental development of the individual and the community." The landscape architect's part in town planning (and his should be a very great rôle indeed) must be one of service to the site and the people who live on it; until now he has been occupied in dispensing decorative favours instead of providing the basis for a new life in Nature.

The green landscape begins where the walls of a building end. But before it has covered many roods there is always a check—a boundary division. A start could be made towards the freeing of the landscape by removing some of the more useless of these barricades.

The communal dwelling clearly calls for the collective garden, which is the first step, but there are not insurmountable difficulties in the way of collective gardens for individual dwellings once their æsthetic and practical advantages are seen. For although the Englishman's home may be his castle, his garden has been known to embrace the co-operative and congenial as well as the feudal and forbidding. A walk through any post-war suburban area will bring to light many community efforts of hedge planting in one variety and

139

of hedge clipping to an approved pattern. Sometimes (this is rare) planting in one garden may echo that in another, but this can usually be ascribed to a more personal relationship than neighbourliness. The latter characteristic is not dead, however, and in the United States, where consciousness of the community spirit of the early settlers has been kept alive, it can be studied much more easily. In the urban residential districts it is uncommon to see boundary fences between the properties in the front. Gardens in the rear are usually fenced and private, but rarely walled. The American regards the man who erects a high wall about his garden almost as a pathological case. Unfortunately this admirable open treatment in American cities with occasional exceptions only serves to reveal a particularly undistinguished native architecture, and it is in Europe that we shall find good architecture and free garden planning closely allied—at Frankfurt-Römerstadt, for example (begun in 1926), an asymmetrically planned estate overlooking the Nidda Valley, where the views are preserved by agricultural zoning. Here and at Neubühl, near Zurich, the front garden for the private dwellings, as a unit, does not exist; roads (free from traffic), verges and approaches are planned and planted as fluidly and simply as possible. The quadrangles and culs-de-sac of the English garden city are absent, but there is no lack of variety, which is provided by the non-axial lay-outs and a variation in the heights of the buildings. At Frankfurt-Römerstadt and Chatenay-Malabry, to mention two fine new towns planned in Europe on the latter practice, dwellings for families with children are planned on two stories and those for artists, married couples, and independent workers in taller blocks. Unstereotyped yet cohesive architectural planning has made the landscape architect's task simpler and the result, particularly at Römerstadt, unusually successful.

These are particular cases of living places planned for special needs. Neubühl has perhaps the characteristics nearest to the present ideas in English progressive housing. Its small regular dwellings with their flat roofs and light-coloured walls might nowadays almost win approval from some progressive council. Yet what chance would these charmingly arranged, collective gardens have of being constructed in this country today except by individual caprice or employer's dictation?* How can ordinary people be made to see the advantages of liberating the garden and thus achieving ordered freedom in their surroundings?

It is a sad fact that fear of order (thought of only in terms of its

* This has always been resented by inhabitants of the model industrial estates, who appear to have developed a dislike for communal gardens because the latter have been forced upon them.

Right, Römerstadt : Allotments separated from flats by drying areas, and overlooking a sterilized zone. Below, Neubühl, Zurich : Family houses and gardens with simple screen hedges and collective planting.

excesses—regimentation and restriction) is a national characteristic, based on our supposed love of liberty. No Englishman has ever evolved anything but an empirical system of philosophy, and not even the idea that to preserve liberty one must plan to defend liberty against licence is good enough to move him. Useless therefore to point out that the engineer provides ordered development in the precise roadway of the housing estate only to find it contradicted by the antagonistic buildings and gardens of the estate itself. An appeal to the commercial instinct, notably stronger than that of liberty, might prove more successful. (Order is profitable; amenities are profitable. The capital appreciation of the first of the new French towns increased in ten years by 800 per cent.*) The competitive instinct might also be developed, but in both cases one cannot help feeling that the method of approach is one to be deplored. A more commendable plan would be to experiment with and put before the public considered practical cases for the communal garden which would act as their own advertisement.

One immediately apparent and seemingly plausible argument against this type of planning is the difficulty of obtaining privacy. Admittedly some form of seclusion is as desirable in the garden as it is in the house itself, but this is quite possible of achievement in almost any communal scheme. The planner's ingenuity has not yet been brought to bear on this problem, which is confused in the public's mind with the question of " privilege " and individual cultivation.

* *Europe Rehoused.* E. Denby.

What the man in the street wants is the right, whether he exercises it or not, to cultivate his own strip of land. The desire for privacy, as evidenced by the universal lack of provision for this amenity in individual gardens all over the country, comes a very long way after this prime consideration.* The introduction of the communal garden (to become, perhaps, the out-of-door social centre and a factor for the improvement of community manners) would be certain to lessen the demand for privacy which is still a universal phobia in our present state of civilization.

* For practical purposes the typical communal garden scheme described in the next chapter embraces the two primary needs: means of obtaining privacy and provision of land for individual cultivation.

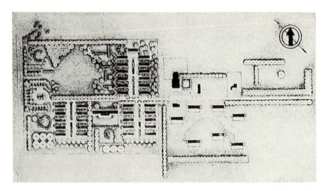

A well-balanced arrangement of gardens in a Farm Security Administration camp in Texas. Landscape architect: Garrett Eckbo.

III—A Solution for Today

It is impossible to imagine the typical neighbourhood garden scheme without also bearing in mind the ideal housing scheme. The garden can no longer be considered a fixed phenomenon with a separate existence—it becomes a variable unit in the sociological pattern. It should no longer be possible to think of gardens without also thinking of schools, shops and welfare centres, as well as houses and apartment blocks. At present, of course, the ideal housing scheme does not exist, and there are differences of opinion over the question of its probable form. Possibly there will never be one ideal housing method, but many ideal schemes. It is certain that gardens need never become stereotyped, although the demands made of them under a new system of housing may be more precise and exacting; it is equally certain that the solution of the housing problem depends to some extent on the evolution of a type more fitting than the present anti-social private garden system.

This system has served its purpose; in the schemes of garden city planners it has proved an insurmountable obstacle to designing for centralization and present-day town planning needs, and is one of the reasons why this school, which is loth to let it pass away, is unable to provide an acceptable solution to national planning problems. In spite of this fact, and although it may be desirable for future development that the system should go, the private garden, or in any case its most valuable features, can and should be retained in one or another different forms, as will be seen.

In the plan illustrated on page 158 are shown the housing requirements of a maximum unit of 6,000 people. The open-air amenities provided include private and communal gardens, allotments, playgrounds for nursery schools, sports fields for junior and senior schools, tennis courts and bowling greens, wading and swimming pools, a plant nursery and glass houses, a small golf course, woodland walks and rides, a boating lake, an open-air theatre and a botanic garden. As well as being considered as units in the scheme, these have been arranged as a related whole and much new landscape planting contributes to the connection between the parts.

On page 145 is a detail of the section of houses for larger families which can be considered in the light of what has been said concerning cultivation and privacy. It embodies a principle which could be

143

applied equally well to gardens for the typical ribbon estate development in evidence all over the country.

It will be seen that consideration of the land between the houses and the approach roads has been omitted. It is assumed that the ubiquitous front garden, which was never anything more than a passage to the house, could seldom be made private, and acted at best as a neat passport to the owner's respectability, has disappeared to make way for an open treatment of the road frontage without divisional barriers. This open treatment, while enabling the land available to be considered as a unified scheme, does not put difficulties in the way of a planting method to mask entrances where desired and to screen windows at a sufficient distance to avoid light exclusion, so that its usefulness is not sacrificed to æsthetic considerations. It is unfortunate that only in a few isolated cases has this form of order been introduced here, and equally unfortunate that under present conditions it can only be satisfactory where some control is exercised—in gated housing estates, for example, such as the one illustrated, where traffic is diluted and upkeep in the hands of a central authority. So long as we line up buildings along corridor roads for through traffic the open treatment will be undesirable except for industrial and administrative development.

Turning to the detail on the opposite page and the space between the two rows of houses usually occupied by private gardens, it is seen that a compromise has been effected by considerably reducing the area of private garden for each house and creating a communal strip between the rows to which each garden has access. There are several good reasons why such a change from the conventional practice is desirable, which it is hoped are made clear in the caption opposite.

The communal garden area is a flexible unit, planned for a variety of needs. Its most useful form would be that of a local park, connected with adjoining park areas, and containing children's swings and play apparatus, paddling pools and seats and benches. In an estate such as the one shown the planting would necessarily be of the simplest character for economy of upkeep, probably consisting of ornamental and shade trees with a few occasional plantations of flowering shrubs in massed arrangements to make for easy cultivation. Large portions of the grass area could be left in a rough state for occasional summer mowing. The whole of the upkeep could be carried out by the tenants or employees of the estate under the direction of a committee whose activities could be decided by the tenants themselves. The committee would have jurisdiction over the functions of the communal areas and the proper conduct of their users. Only co-operative effort can achieve the common garden and ensure its permanent value.

144

THE MINIMUM GARDEN

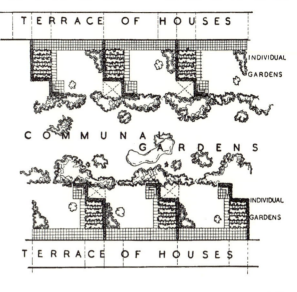

Gardens are usually too large for their owners to look after, yet never large enough to satisfy their need for space and exercise. Both of these disadvantages are removed in the creation of the Minimum Garden. The private garden thus evolved is small enough to be worked by any owner and will give him more pleasure than a much larger area, which would inevitably lack the necessary care. His need for space and freedom is supplied by the extension of his own private garden into the landscape. These gardens contain a terrace under the house windows, a rectangular lawn, a sheltered recess for tables and chairs, a space for children's sandpit, play-room or toolshed, flower beds, and a screen planting of flowering trees and shrubs. To obtain coherence the structure of all the gardens is the same, leaving the owner free to exercise his individual horticultural taste in the planting. Similarly, the position of the seating recess and the play space could be reversed when the aspect was unfavourable to the former and the tree and shrub planting varied to provide the requisite height and density for screening. The similarity in the plans ensures equal protection for each unit and the screen trees at the end of the gardens, besides forming the boundary and the main planting of the communal strip, serve an especially useful purpose as a break between the rows of buildings.

Logically enough, this method of garden planning bears some relation to the planning of interiors. The Minimum Garden is, in fact, an extension of the house : an out-of-door living room, planned by the landscape architect and decorated to a greater or lesser degree by the owner.

Garden furniture and flowers in the frame of beds could be introduced as desired, so that the garden need never become an impersonal thing or a mere copy of its neighbour.

The system described (it is only a particular method for a special problem) provides these amenities: First, a private family area small enough to be cultivated by the individual, yet large enough for the family's immediate needs; second, a communal area linked to larger areas and cultivated collectively. As outlined so far it does not provide allotments for vegetable cultivation, nor any form of recreational grounds apart from the needs of the immediate family and neighbourhood group.

The latter requirements are provided in the larger scheme, where approximately eleven acres of allotment gardens and fourteen acres of sports ground are shown, in addition to school gardens and playgrounds. The owners of the private gardens already mentioned are provided for in the allotment space, although this would normally be about eighteen acres for a housing unit of six thousand people. It is assumed that a proportion only of the holders of private gardens would require additional land.

In considering the needs of dwellers in the multi-storey buildings, however, allotments must take a place of first importance. A change from the current allotment policy should be encouraged and the plots brought within the community's fold instead of being located at a distance from the dwelling. In certain new housing schemes this has been done. At Römerstadt, for example, the area has been reserved directly under the walls of the apartment blocks, and the result has been a marked improvement in the standard of cultivation and the general appearance of the whole. In the present scheme the allotment area has been placed between the flat and single-family units to allow for convenient access from each, but in crowded areas, where space is valuable, allotment areas might well be arranged as at Römerstadt instead of invariably being ousted in favour of dreary wastes of civic planting. Deprive the flat dweller of his right to cultivate the soil and you rob him of a cherished and precious liberty, as well as a prime factor in his or her mental and physical well-being. If allotments were called "gardens for intensive cultivation" (le Corbusier), released from the tainted atmosphere of the gasworks, and their cultivators given reasonable facilities for enjoying them at their own doorstep, there is no telling what difference might be made to the social life of any community.

Another real problem connected with multiple housing is that of recreational areas for children. Authorities in London and other large towns are faced with this question, which is often answered by locking children behind iron railings in asphalted areas from which they can only be released by the keeper's key. In Russia, where children have more freedom and are at liberty to run where they please, the resulting noise is distressing to European temperaments other than the Slav, on which it appears to have a tonic effect. There would, however, seem to be a solution to the difficulty of reducing noise and yet keeping play spaces at a convenient distance from the dwelling. In the scheme illustrated a form of building is used which allows the living space to run east and west, leaving the end walls free of windows. The play space is situated at the south end of each building, and is provided with shelters and covered areas for floor games, as well as the out-of-door apparatus usually included. With a part of the area surfaced to carry off storm water, playgrounds are much more capable

A ride on the Claremont estate. To the extreme left is a specimen of Abies brachyphylla, *the Nikko fir. Beyond it is one of* Cryptomeria japonica. *Both of these were planted in the last third of the nineteenth century, the cedar of Lebanon to the right of the photograph being an earlier eighteenth-century contribution.*

of satisfying the child's needs than roof gardens, which are advocated for this purpose by some authorities (quite apart from questions of space) for smaller children. The child prefers contact with the ground, and roof gardens would seem to be more suitable for the aged, infirm and generally less active section of the population.

It will be obvious to those who have read these pages that communal landscape planning must be regulated by zoning methods as rigorous as those for industrial or domestic planning. It should be a part of the complete neighbourhood unit, to which it can contribute in great measure a tangible organic form. For instance, in the scheme illustrated there are considerations besides those connected with transport for grouping the buildings at the end of the estate nearest the business and shopping centre on the old meadow land. They are considerations which involve (1) preserving the historical mansion and the landscape garden surrounding it from encroaching buildings; (2) preserving the eighteenth-century wood containing many rare trees of unique botanical interest; (3) giving the public access to the most interesting parts of the estate without detriment to the social life of the dwellers on the estate itself; and (4) providing those dwellers with the largest possible open space compatible with rational housing conditions and site requirements.

Here all this is possible without the loss of a single tree. In an estate containing the finest specimens in the country of the papaw,* sassafras, and Kentucky coffee† trees, as well as magnificent examples

* " Of interest botanically as the only hardy plant of its natural order." *Trees and Shrubs Hardy in the British Isles.* W. J. Bean. John Murray. 5th Edition, 1929.

† ". . . Foliage perhaps the most beautiful of all hardy trees." *Ibid.*

147

of cedar, cunninghamia, sequoia and other luxuriant evergreens, such zoning would seem to be well worth while. Generally, the fact that a forest tree often requires a hundred years or more to take on a mature loveliness is worth more consideration than the thought that " only God " can make it. A tree renews its vital forces annually, and with skilled attention its life can often be indefinitely prolonged. One wonders whether the many societies which exist to schedule old buildings for preservation would have a tittle of public value beside a society formed to schedule noble plant forms of historical and botanical interest. A point in favour of rational architectural and landscape planning is that its machinery acts to preserve and develop Nature's material for the people, in contrast to the sterile preservationist mechanism of many existing planning institutions. It seems a more valuable social contribution to provide the means for a life in Nature, rather than a life spent in sentimental contemplation of her far-off beauties. A landscape zoned for use, to flow uninterrupted from doorstep to open country, would be worth preserving; but to make it possible, instead of erecting new barriers, we must break the old ones down. The communal garden would make a valuable beginning, for inevitably it would point the way to the creation of the communal landscape.

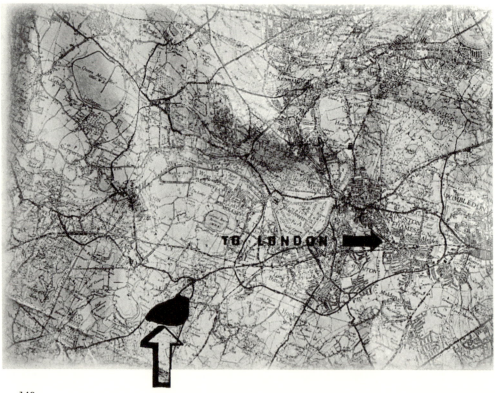

A GARDEN LANDSCAPE IN TRANSITION

Claremont, Surrey

*Above, the park gates, with a view of the planted landscape.
Top, the drive is about three-quarters of a mile long and leads
up to the house which, says Brayley, " occupies a commanding
eminence near the middle of the park, and forms an oblong
square, measuring forty-five yards by thirty-four." Opposite,
map showing the site.*

In 1770 Claremont was an undulating park of 284 acres (fifteen miles from Hyde
Park Corner), as laid out by Kent and " improved " by Capability Brown. The brick-
walled garden to the north-east of the house is an earlier relic and has been ascribed
to Vanbrugh. The site was left open to the north-east and a wood planted to the

Above, the west front. The finest cedars are quite close to the house, which is entirely surrounded by lawns. To its right is the tree-covered mount on which is an observatory tower erected by the first owner, the Earl of Clare, " the situation being singularly romantic," as Campbell said, " and from the high tower has a most prodigious fine prospect of the Thames." Right, a corner of the lake, with its surround of trees and rhododendrons.

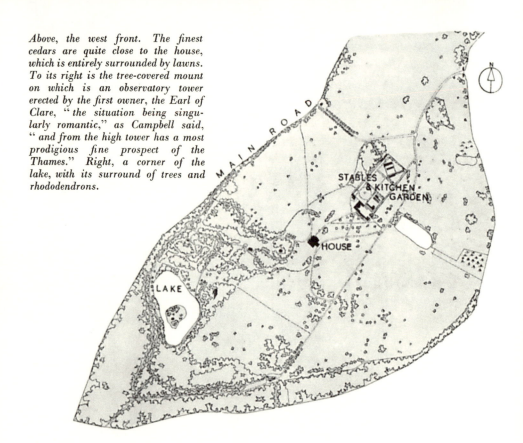

PLAN 1816. POPULATION 40.

south-west. The lake of six and a half acres is in the pre-serpentine landscape style and has an island graced by a typical Brown pavilion (now in ruins). Narrow carriage drives wound through the estate and gravel paths gave access to the wood. In 1816 the house became a royal residence and much additional planting was carried out. In the main the landscape style was adhered to, and flowers were never allowed outside the walled garden, which, however, contains some fine specimen trees. In the heart
150

WHAT DO
THE PEGS MARK?

of the wood is an elegant camellia house, now rapidly approaching collapse. Time has made curious changes—a grassy platform raised to afford a view of the water now looks over an uneven tabletop of trees and includes the unusual sight of five cedars planted in a clump. The rhododendron planting added in the latter half of the nineteenth century has formed a magnificent undergrowth to the wood, framed the walks and provided a cascade of early summer blossom by the side of the lake.

On hallowed ground. A new house built within the original brick-walled garden.

PLAN 1938

POPULATION 800

Stereotyped avenue planting on an estate road.

In the 1920's the estate was sold to a number of speculative builders. Only part of the housing development shown in the plan on this page has been carried out (open space is shown grey, enclosure white) the remainder being either scheduled for building in the near future or held up for reasons unknown. The wood is as yet untouched except at its extreme north-east and south-west corners. and is of extraordinary interest from a horticultural point of view. The old mansion has become a *de luxe* girls' school.

152

[Continued on page 155]

Diverse architectural styles contribute towards uniform planning messiness, a state of things not improved by unco-ordinated garden lay-outs.

Right, laying down a new landscape at Claremont today. Concrete garden pools in the grounds of a recently completed house.

TO VANBRUGH, KENT AND BROWN

This obelisk, which once embellished the park, now stands in the kitchen garden of a house. Claremont, departing as a piece of landscape, has returned to a well-wooded situation suitable for highly eligible building sites. The inexorable process will probably never be better illustrated than in this picture, with the Agent's TO BE SOLD board standing cheek by jowl with the monument whose inscription, almost illegible, commemorates the activities in one park of three of the greatest names in English landscape architecture, Sir John Vanbrugh, William Kent and Lancelot Brown.

154

THE BUTCHER METHOD

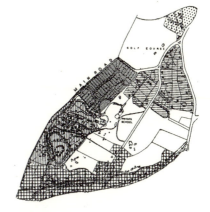

Developed by five distinct firms of builders, the extent of whose operations to date is shown in the plan above, the Claremont Estate was inevitably cut up into small enclosures, a process which will no doubt continue until there is nothing left to cut up. Thus, despite all the developers can do to retain the amenities (and they have tried hard), the real amenity, represented by the free landscape of Kent and Brown, is destroyed.

THE NEW INCLOSURE
[WHITE REPRESENTS OPEN SPACE. BLACK, INCLOSURE]

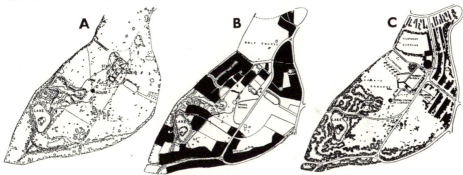

In place of the old landlord's inclosure there is taking place all over the countryside a new and more concentrated form of inclosure which in parcelling the landscape into minute private properties is acting more seriously against the interests of the community than did the old. Estates such as Claremont, A, are becoming permanently sterilized as built-over areas, B, while with a rational planning of the whole area, and the concentration of dwellings in certain parts of it, more people might be housed yet and virtually the whole estate might be left open for the benefit of the residents and public, C.

Of the housing little need be said except that it belongs to the £2,000-£5,000 (1939) type of development. The style is mainly " Surrey Tudor," and the most exclusive house on the estate is one which has squeezed itself inside Vanbrugh's kitchen garden (marked A on page 152). Prices vary little in each section, which appears illogical; a plot containing a cedar, a cunninghamia, two redwoods and a copper beech, would seem to be a choicer pitch than one containing a few firs and the foundations of a

[Continued on page 158]

SUGGESTED
RE-DEVELOPMENT

A modern dormitory town for London, without the disadvantages of Howard's "town-country" (the inevitable result of land subdivision). Remember that this estate is fifteen miles from Hyde Park Corner. Hence the suggested re-development allows for flats as well as terrace houses. By this means 6,000 people could be housed in the northern end of the park. (The lay-out is shown in the plan on page 158). The space between the flats and the allotments is occupied by children's play gardens which are separated from the latter by a belt of trees. These screen from the flats the allotment huts and storage rooms, which are intended to offer also the out-of-door resting place usually provided by the summer house. The road in the foreground leads from the housing area to the schools and playgrounds. Some measure of formality is observed in the planting along the roads, but continuous avenues would be avoided. The coming of education and amusement centres is accompanied by a freedom of planning which is made possible by the intercommunication of the lives of those who would live here. This town-planning problem is uncomplicated by the question of industry or transport, which would presumably be one for the adjoining built-up area to which it is linked.

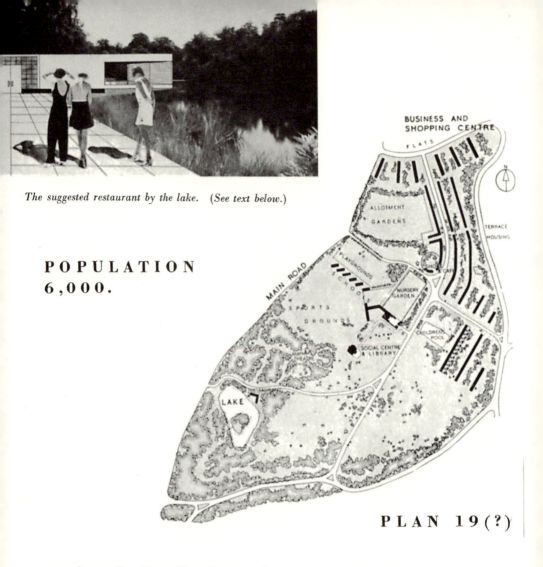

The suggested restaurant by the lake. (*See text below.*)

POPULATION
6,000.

BUSINESS AND
SHOPPING CENTRE

FLATS

ALLOTMENT

GARDENS

TERRACE
HOUSING

MAIN ROAD

PLAYGROUNDS

SCHOOL

NURSERY
GARDEN

SPORTS

GROUNDS

CHILDREN'S
POOL

SOCIAL CENTRE
& LIBRARY

THEATRE

LAKE

PLAN 19(?)

mausoleum.   But this is still the Romantic Age, and it may be that the ancient monument will prove the greater attraction of the two.

With housing concentrated in blocks of flats on the rising ground to the north-east and in terraces of single family dwellings; with shops, schools, cafés, library and social centre provided for the immediate needs of the neighbourhood unit, and with facilities for all important forms of out-of-door recreation . . . riding, walking, boating, swimming, field games, and horticultural pursuits, a form of planning is evolved which serves the inhabitants, the public and the interests of preservation for future generations.   The wood and lake (in all about 100 acres) are accessible to the public by a separate entrance from the main road and a restaurant and swimming pool built for their convenience.   The wood also contains an open-air stage in an existing amphitheatre, picnic-grounds, and an observatory in the eighteenth-century prospect tower. The housing unit is surrounded by communal parks and gardens and is provided with children's playgrounds, allotment areas and sports grounds.   The panoramic views from the house (used as a museum, library and social centre) are preserved and new landscape planting in connection with road and housing development is carried out in the park.   The kitchen garden of six acres (too small for market work) is a nursery garden for the estate, which has its own horticultural and landscape committee connected with a members' club.   The latter institution, besides being of social value, ensures a controlled and uniform planting of the estate.   All development is thus co-ordinated to produce an open landscape, despite the fact that the site now houses 6,000 people in place of 800.

158

IV—The Wider Planning

Landscape architecture has grown up with the present century. Like town planning, its value is being recognized only when unchecked development has considerably restricted its opportunity for social amelioration, but the need for an ordered countryside appears now to be apparent even to those who still wish to sterilize vast areas of it for their own class and its activities, and some form of landscape planning seems not only necessary but imminent.

Ought we to be surprised by the fact that in the short fifty years or so of its existence civic landscape architecture has become hoary with tradition in the manner of garden planning? It seems not, for that period saw the triumph of the Holy Italian revival which still drives its axial shafts into the mind of the architectural designer. The clichés of the École des Beaux Arts are hard to disestablish, and the uncomprehending attitude to Nature apparent in the Philistinism which passes for town planning has meant that through the years the latter activity has ignored the human scale. The dominance of the drawing board in all forms of architecture has prevented society from being given what it needs, though not, doubtless, what it deserves, especially in city squares and public gardens.

The other false tradition in landscape architecture is that of the "natural garden." We have seen how the *laissez-faire* school of garden planners developed and what happened to the landscape garden in the nineteenth century. Though completely dismembered in the meticulous Victorian carving-up, some fragments are preserved

159

The work of the engineer in the landscape. Châtelard
Aqueduct (1926) by the Swiss designer, Robert Maillart.

in the landscape park, which is still a perfect caged example of the landscape design of sixty to eighty years ago. Many of the London parks have escaped the Italian influence, which is strongest in the north; with their neat iron railings, showy summer bedding displays and massive plantations of evergreens they remain a pleasant oleograph, and never having been designed primarily for recreation, cannot be condemned on the score that they are no longer useful. As museum pieces they undoubtedly increase in value yearly, but the pity of it is that the school of planners which they represent would keep alive the tradition of these antiques. For the Brownists are at large today, grading and contouring, and smoothing and shaping—through man's handiwork striving to obliterate the work of man.

How unfitting for contemporary needs is the work of these two schools is clearly shown when they attempt a solution to new landscape problems. Roadway planting is one of these which both the Italianate and natural protagonists have taken upon themselves to tackle. The first is prone to make of every byway a ceremonial avenue, with regimented tree planting lining thoroughfares along which no procession is ever destined to pass. The second, more subtle yet all the more insidious in its power to blight, would follow the engineer along the arterial road, obscure the significance of his bold cuttings with a cover of arboreal growth, and emasculate the surrounding landscape with the products of the florist's window. Having learned to plant, the landscape gardeners now plant without restraint.

Both schools have powerful allies. When the honest countryman complains that " he doesn't like bypass roads," one can be certain the local preservation society has had a word in his ear. Deprecating the work of the engineer, whose activities are perhaps the greatest contribution made to the landscape in the last one hundred years, is an unfortunate and shortsighted policy. Well meaning though the industrious preservation societies undoubtedly are, some of us would believe that they meant better by the countryside if the offending word " preservation " were struck out of their titles and a more comprehensive adjective inserted in its place. In the long run, to preserve carefully is less worthy an object than to create wisely, and in the landscape sterilization can only act as a brake on progress towards effective planning.

And so these false traditions slow progress to the measure of a pigmy's tread. But there is luckily another and a more vital tradition for the new art, a tradition of work done unostentatiously and with care—of seventeenth-century farm-owners hedging enclosed landscapes into ordered ribbons and squares, of eighteenth-century landscapists merging house and garden with plantations and lawns into the countryside, and of nineteenth-century plantsmen patiently evolving a race of hardy plants to decorate and enliven the created scene. These are the worthwhile manifestations of our tradition—a tradition which gives us a root in the past to enable our own growth to flower more gratefully in the present.

If the traditionally worthless can be kept apart from the worthwhile, there is hope for regaining order in the countryside. But not the old order, nor that defined by those people in whose power it lies to make a beginning. To them *organization* still means the parcelling out of the landscape into plots in garden cities, *nature* a refuge from the city in national parks and coastal reservations untouched by the

K   161 hand of man, and *art* a statue standing in a civic square. Art training for the planner is the glorification of the academic tradition, and the sociological sense is developed in him only sufficiently to enable him to tackle the problem of housing a population which gravitates towards new and unplanned industrial centres.

What sense is there in such an attitude? Why sterilize vast areas of the countryside and turn vaster areas into the primæval jungle of decentralized, unplanned building development, when one solution of the problem is ready to hand in the multiple dwelling? Having sterilized the countryside in the form of national and regional parks,* how is it proposed to keep the natural scene free from contamination by art or from interference by planners? The promoters of the scheme have put it abroad that they wish " to maintain landscape beauties,"† but make no mention of creating new ones. Perhaps, they suggest, the landscape architect might be admitted to perform the operation of plastic surgery—to patch up the scar of an old quarry, for instance, by planting it with trees " to hide the work of man." But, they warn us, there must be no interference with Nature. There must be roads, of course, and perhaps wardens' huts and hostels for walkers whose communion with wild Nature has made them oblivious to time and the way home. Even a petrol station or two is advised for the motorist who has forgotten to fill up at the park entrance, but there must be no development. Nature must reign unspoilt and inviolate. There must be nothing to " spoil the view."

Is it not yet conceivable that a well-designed and well-placed building, a bridge or road, can be an addition rather than a menace to the countryside? The truth is that where the public is admitted and encouraged art and architecture come, too, and none of the preservation schemes will be of use without them. Keeping areas of the countryside free from the horror of unplanning is not enough. For these parks to be valuable, they must cater for the needs of the community. Besides existing as a breeding ground for wild life, these areas will become a playground for the people, who will demand the amenities of life in the form of buildings for the supply of food and

* " The Case for National Parks in Great Britain," by the Standing Committee on National Parks. 1938.

† Those who have studied the distribution of plant life on the earth's surface and the evolution of our present countryside will understand that a " landscape strictly preserved in its natural aspects " is a contradiction in terms. Nature is continually changing; organic life is a continuous process of growth and decay, and to preserve any one aspect of a natural scene involves perpetual and arduous interference on the part of man. Apart from this, only the waste lands and the remotest peaks and foreshores of Great Britain can be called " natural " in both origin and development.

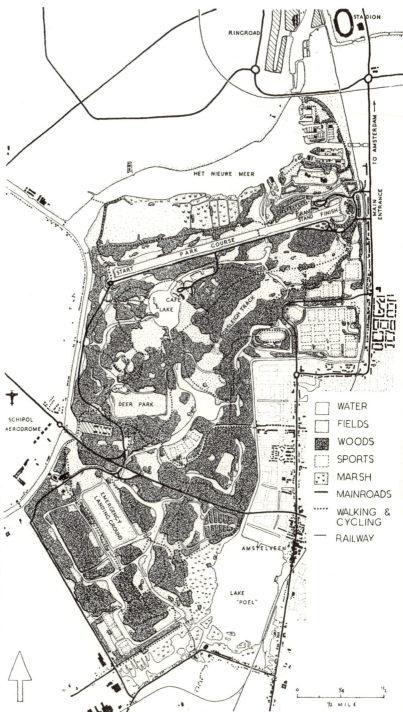

RINGROAD

STADION

TO AMSTERDAM

MAIN ENTRANCE

HET NIEUWE MEER

GRAND STAND FINISH

START

PARK COURSE

CAFÉ LAKE

BOBSLEIGH TRACK

DEER PARK

SCHIPOL AERODROME

EMERGENCY LANDING GROUND

AMSTELVEEN

LAKE "POEL"

	WATER
	FIELDS
■	WOODS
	SPORTS
	MARSH
—	MAINROADS
⋯	WALKING & CYCLING
—	RAILWAY

Plan of the new Amsterdam park designed by the architect C. van Eesteren and his associates in the Public Works Department. It occupies an area about equal in size to Richmond Park or the Bois de Boulogne. In its layout, devoid of traditional clichés, van Eesteren may be said to have produced the modernist's challenge in this branch of landscape design.

0   ¼   ½
½ MILE

163

shelter, pleasure beaches and games areas. Create for them a free and rational architecture which expresses the liberty of their minds and bodies and fulfils their social needs. Let them have cleanliness, light and air, and the spaciousness of good indoor and outdoor designing. Let them have the stimulus of an open, varied, enjoyable countryside. Clear, build, preserve and plant for them; above all, plan for them.

The creative attitude could be extended to the countryside surrounding these reservations, to the land around our homes and workplaces. It could benefit not only the nation's playgrounds, but the nation's factories and workshops. The liberating influence of open spaces and communal gardens flowing through these developed areas, a continuous stream of verdure, would be more satisfying than any of the so-called " beautification " schemes (which demand extreme decentralization to be effective, and are therefore wasteful when possible at all) and even more valuable than a " green belt," since it would start from the doorstep and grow outwards to the open countryside. Such centralization and such an open treatment can become the nucleus of a new landscape, beautiful and satisfying in all its parts, and not merely in areas too remote to be accessible, or which unplanning and chaos have not yet reached.

Let the people have a pleasaunce round their homes and the desire for far-off earthly paradises, untouched by the hand of man, will disappear. Across the mountain top and through the jungle we walk on city streets, bearing with us our personal fragment of civilization wherever we go. If that fragment is a pleasant memory it will help us to understand and enjoy the real Nature, not as an illusion, but as a mirror of ourselves.

And so, as has already been pointed out, in planning the countryside for work and play the garden must be given a foremost place. It is a vision for our guidance—*exitis in paradisum*. A thousand years ago the garden was a paradise in men's minds; today, more urgently, this vision should become a reality.

In the present search for a new ideal the conventional garden must be forgotten. Whereas in the Dark Ages the garden was bounded by the cloister walls, today not even Laurin's silken cord need bind it. The units of the landscape can be interlinked; areas reserved for industry and agriculture can be parted to make way for the flow of the landscape, used for rest and recreation. A revolution in design must free it from the styles. It must be released from the dominance of straight-lined avenues of trees, symbols of civic pomp and arrogance; from beautification which exists only to obscure the ugliness which lies behind; from the cramping and torturing of plant material. Instead,

Top, the Amsterdam Bosch plan lying between built-up areas on the outskirts of the old city.

Bottom, part of the boat-race course appears to the left of this illustration, and in the foreground one of the yachting lakes and the main restaurant.

K*

let plant forms in harmony with site and purpose be used in simple fluid patterns, in economy of design and restful ordered schemes. Let the life of the plant in its character, placing and usefulness for sheltering and screening provide a stimulus for the life of man. With man's knowledge, skill and art, Nature can perform the function which the modern world requires of her; free planning in building and landscape is the ideal, and a co-operation between planners essential to its attainment. The town planner as co-ordinator cannot do without the help of the landscape architect, the engineer, and the architect, whose functions through the years have become inter-dependent and interwoven.

In a sick and suffering world the first profession is as important as the last, and we have come to realize that the earthly paradise is unobtainable without the planner of garden and landscape. Society cannot afford to overlook his power to contribute to the life of the community. In his own medium he dispenses the two chief anodynes of life—art and play—without which we perish as surely as if we lack bread. That medium, the landscape, has taken on a new meaning which he alone, with his own special art and knowledge, can make especially clear to us. Let us give him the opportunity for creation.

And here must end this exposition of a new approach to garden and landscape planning, two aspects of one major art of the twentieth century. The eighteenth century brought the landscape into garden planning; the twentieth century must bring the garden into the landscape. Through such a progress can arise the humanized land-scape, the social conception of the countryside, and the garden of tomorrow.

MODERN
AMERICAN
GARDENS

The pages which follow are a pictorial sampling of modern work in the United States. Although it is impossible to give more than the barest glimpse, regional differences in plant and structural material will be noticeable and help to lend a variety to the scenes they compose. It is too soon to discern any distinct stylistic innovations; and it may be that in a country so vast they will never exert the influence that, say, Le Corbusier has had on American building. The author's own work has been done in the Eastern States and he has included examples from California and elsewhere. The desert country is represented by Frank Lloyd Wright, an architect who loves plants but seldom has the opportunity to use them in his own inimitable way.

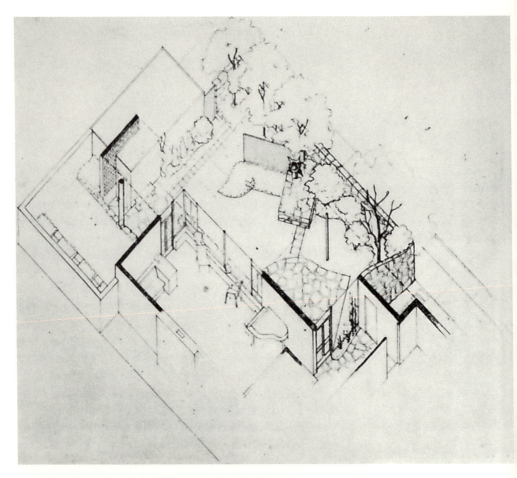

On this and the facing page are illustrations of a very small garden made to appear larger by diagonal emphasis. The wooden objects were designed by Christopher Tunnard after meeting Paul Nash in England. Garden at 4, Buckingham Street, Cambridge, Mass. Architects: Stone & Koch. Landscape architect: Christopher Tunnard.

Top left, outdoor living area. The paved terrace is afforded complete overhead protection by the bedroom wing. There is a roof deck over the living room. Bottom left, the yard from the canopied space between the house and the garage. The screen is introduced to break the rectangular enclosure of the small courtyard. Right, three detail views of the garden. The ground surfaces are grass, white marble chips, purple granite, concrete paving blocks and bluestone. The wooden feature to the left of the screen is an " objet trouvé " of surrealist invention. There are several of these in unexpected places in the garden.

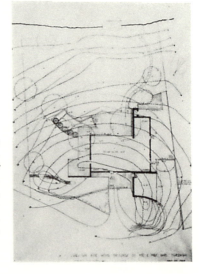

Top and centre, views of a large landscaped garden at Lincoln, Mass., in wooded country near Thoreau's Walden Pond, showing the treatment of the terrace. Top, the terrace looking towards the house. Centre, a view of the garden shelter from the house. Right, plan of a suburban garden at Winchester, Mass. Here there is very little planting— just earth moving, terraces, and lawns down to the lake. Architect for both houses: G. Holmes Perkins. Landscape architect: Christopher Tunnard.

170

Travelling over miles of desert outside Phœnix, Arizona, one reaches this oasis—but not quite an oasis, since desert plants have been used to create the landscape. Taliesin West, Phœnix, Arizona. Architect: Frank Lloyd Wright.

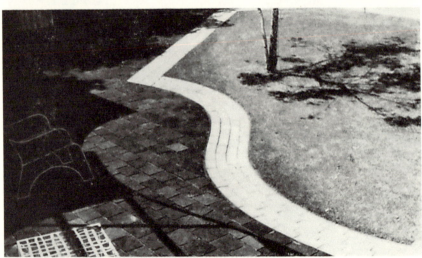

Garden at the San Francisco World Fair, 1939, by Thomas Church. Top, redwood paving: centre, redwood blocks and white brick paving: left, the transite screen.

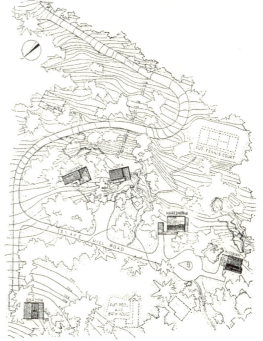

Right, plan of a small house development at Belmont, Mass. Architect: Carl Koch. Landscape architect: Christopher Tunnard. Above, a student project at Harvard, under the direction of Walter Bogner and Christopher Tunnard, for a new community at Lincoln, Mass.

Above left, model of a proposed new wing and garden for the Museum of Modern Art, New York. Architect: Philip L. Godwin. Landscape architect: Christopher Tunnard. Above right, a sketch of the garden looking east away from the Museum. In the foreground is the Lehmbruck Standing Youth (1913), a gift to the Museum's permanent collection by Mrs. John D. Rockefeller. In the middle distance on a pedestal in the pool among the fountain jets is the Lachaise Floating Figure (1927) in bronze, given anonymously in memory of the artist. The garden is completely redesigned to harmonize with the proposed structural alterations to the Museum. Left, view of a terrace in the garden of James Thrall Soby at Farmington, Connecticut, designed by the author. The wing to the right is a gallery for modern paintings by the architect Henry-Russell Hitchcock. There is a swimming pool and large free-standing mobile by Alexander Calder.

THE MODERN GARDEN
by Joseph Hudnut
Dean of Harvard University

Since men, from the beginning of recorded history, and no doubt long before, have striven to reshape both shelter and the environment of shelter in accordance with a spiritual need—since these have always been, not the consequences of biological necessity merely, but also at all times materials for expression—I see no reason to suppose that modern man will not desire to build, not only his house, but equally his garden in accordance with his inward promptings. I must confess that I am somewhat surprised to be told again and again that an impulse so old and universal will be frustrated by the difficulty of using new techniques and materials in the garden or because Nature has failed to break down those climatic barriers which localize plant materials or to hasten that slow evolution by which new plants are developed.

Certainly the garden architects who created Caprarola and Vaux-le-Vicomte and Stowe did not demand of Nature that she should throw away her ancient palette of foliage, hill, and stream, to seek out for them new inventions. The invention was theirs, I think, not Nature's. When they looked into the heart of their time and made it visible—now in magnificent theatres for Renaissance pageantry, now in the Cartesian discipline which reflected eighteenth-century France, and now in the lush sentiment with which Jean-Jacques Rousseau suffused the landscapes of England—they yet placed no rigorous strain upon the bounty of Nature. Neither did they demand of architects as a prerequisite for expression a new vocabulary of structural forms and materials.

I am impatient with those garden architects who attempt to create a new form of garden by no other means than the introduction of novel constructions or unusual plant forms. I find somewhat boring, after the first surprise, those tubular metal seats " designed for mass construction," those gazebos on iron stilts, those intricately formed beds and boxes outlined in concrete, and all those accessories in paving, furniture, and lighting intended as unmistakable assertions of modernity. One may, of course, obtain a certain congruity between house and garden by carrying out the garden accessories in materials identical to those used in the house. But this congruity cannot have any lasting or convincing character if the adaptation of the garden ends here. It takes more than a lily to make a Chinese lady.

I am equally out of sympathy with those architects who propose the abandonment of all attempts at garden form in the landscape setting of the modern house. The much-quoted remark of Professor Henry-Russell Hitchcock echoes this feeling: " The important principle is the preservation of all possible values previously in existence in the landscape setting "—the garden architect is to add only the simplest and most practical provision for specific human needs, a key-note echoed by Mr. Richard Neutra who says that the essential characteristic of the modern house is friendliness to the out-of-doors, a " generous opening to health agents and a biologically minded appreciation of the soil in which all life is rooted."

This theory, which is not devoid of romantic overtones, seems to me to be more persuasive in the words of philosophers than in the practice of garden architects. The fact that gardens are something more than extensions of nature is a fact too often confirmed by experience to be dissipated by even the most skilful of dialectics. A meadow with a house in it is not the same as a meadow without a house, whatever may be the " friendliness " of the house to the outdoors; the values of the meadow are certainly altered by this intrusion, even though the house conform in the strictest fashion to biological necessity. Art instantly alters the pattern of its environment. Cataracts, cliffs, and forest vistas assume a tamer aspect through a contact with humanity; trees crowd more sweetly into a shade when they enfold a fragment of human culture; nor is there any element of the knowable universe which does not assume a new quality when measured against the tenancy of man. Certainly a harmony between the modern house and its site is more evident when the site, like the house, has escaped both romance and an oppressive formality; but a deep or persuasive unity cannot be attained when one and not the other has submitted to a conscious control of form. Therefore I do not despair of gardens which are, like houses, *designed*. Around our new architecture, which will be increasingly intellectualized, a discipline will still be imposed upon plants, contours, and accessories; indeed I think that this will be made more rather than less stringent. Some organic relation between house and garden is imperative and this common organism must be conditioned not merely upon the visible world but upon the energies of the human spirit—a spirit which, fortunately, is not conformable to every aspect of the non-human world.

We must continue our search for some basis of formalization if we are to create a garden for the modern house. Perhaps we can discover this basis within the house: some principle of order which, extended beyond its walls, is destined to overcome the order, or disorder, of its surroundings. One such principle at least has been suggested: that very provocative principle which is called *functionalism*. Whatever æsthetic meanings are discoverable in the modern house, these were developed, it is believed, from a useful disposition of space and structure; may we not, then, discover analagous meanings—or create them—from the useful features of the site ? A garden is a useful place: a place in which to rest, to entertain, to exercise, to play. The useful elements of the garden, like the useful elements of the house, can—it is said—be made the source of contemplative as well as practical delights.

Necessity first charted the form that gardens took: the necessity for protection against marauding beasts which brought the enclosing wall; the necessity for irrigation which brought water-courses into the garden scheme; the necessity for giving certain kinds of plants the environments under which they thrive, which brought arbours and shaded areas. Out of these simple adaptations grew the main elements which figure in garden designs even today. As we look over the garden architect's wide vocabulary of forms, we find scarcely one that has not a homely paternity. Arbours and orchards, groves and hedges, orangeries, aviaries and dovecotes, gateways, walls and stairs: each lovely ornament the garden wears dropped in her lap from some—pragmatic—head. We can, therefore, readily persuade ourselves that the modern gardener will find ample precedent for beginning his work with those new facilities which are addressed to the uses of contemporary life, confident in the knowledge that many a noble lineage sprung from as rude an ancestry. If the inherited forms which exist " for their own sake " unjustified by practical purpose and which clutter up the site with a tiresome fussiness must give way to utilitarian forms—to the rigid mechanical forms of tennis court and swimming pool, to concrete terraces, those " convenient outdoor living-spaces," to the drying-yard and the garage, to regimented vegetables and roses grown like gooseberries—history nevertheless sanctions a faith that these may in time become sources of a discreet and carefully cultivated delight.

Now there can be no doubt of the importance of modern utilities as æsthetic elements opposite to contemporary life, but it may be doubted if their presence is sufficient for the important intentions of modern design. Practical requirements, like structural elements, are means, not ends, in modern architecture. Because they are functional, that is to say, moulded by the attitudes and movements of our own society, these forms will receive more intimately whatever ideal of form is peculiar to our day; but it is that ideal, and not the utilities, which is the true substance of architecture.

Our gardens, like our houses, must indeed be conditioned upon use. They must be conditioned also upon topography and techniques, and they must take into account the need of men for play and for illusion; but if they are to attain any enduring command of our imaginations, they must also be conditioned upon qualities more universal in character. They must conform to our vision of the world and to our need for order and completeness in that world. There are no processes of rationalization which are likely to eradicate from men the desire to translate into their environment this spiritual need. The shape and arrangement of the site, no less than the constructed forms of the house, will—if subject to our control—proclaim that ancient aspiration. The modern man, like his forbears, will remake nature in his own image.

We have misunderstood the modern house if we have not discovered in it some hint of this universal quality. The modern house is not merely a protest; it is also an adventure. The liberating spirit which invades this machine is creating an ideal of form not less strenuous than that which is overcome. This free disposition of spaces, lightly confined by thin contours, which answer so intimately the pressures and directions of our society, is as surely subjected to an intellectual discipline as was the classicism which it displaces. These rooms that throw open their walls to admit through wide areas of glass the light and freedom of the out-of-doors are as rigorously conditioned upon a search for expression. If roofs are made flat and floors carried on metal columns and not on masonry, if walls are displaced by thin membranes of wood or plaster hung like curtains on a metallic framework, if surfaces inside and out are clear of ornament and shadow, this is not to be explained as merely boredom with the antique attitudes, nor as caprice intent on " something different " ; still less as the necessary operation of a scientific law. This informality, precision and clarity, this delight in mechanical servants and in forms meticulously adapted to function, this exploitation of new materials and processes, this crystalline elegance of form and of plane: these are not merely the expressions of science, of efficiency, of hygiene; they are the elements of a new æsthetic.

I am inclined to believe that this æsthetic is most clearly exhibited in the *new quality of space* and in the new command of space: a space free as in no other architecture from the tyranny of structure. In our new houses structure exists not to confine space but to model it, to direct its flow, to define the volumes into which it is only lightly divided. It is these volumes which are the important elements of our design; and we are as free to arrange them as a sculptor is free to evoke from inert stone his patterns of solid shapes. Our arrangements of space will be less evidently the consequence of geometric principles; they will rely less upon balance, proportion, symmetrical rhythms; their separation from the outward cosmic space will be less definite; but they will escape, nevertheless, purely functional adaptations. From their exactitude of definition, from their triumph over gravity, from their inexhaustible variety in shape and relationship, and from the consequent freedom in the relations of distances, the ordering of intervals, the harmony or contrast of measured or dissonant volumes, there has been created a new material of expression whose range and resourcefulness we have until now scarcely guessed at.

177

Gardens, like houses, are built of space. Gardens are fragments of space set aside by the planes of terraces and walls and disciplined foliage. Until now we have defined too nicely the differences between that space which is roofed and within the house and that which is left outside and around the house. We did not see, until the architect threw down his walls, that the space of house and that of garden are parts of a single organism: that the secret of unity lies in a unity of spatial sequences. The new vision has dissolved the ancient boundary between architecture and landscape architecture. The garden flows into and over the house: through loggias and courts and wide areas of clear glass, and over roofs and sun-rooms and canopied terraces. The house reaches out into the garden with walls and terraced enclosures that continue its rhythms and share its grace. The concordant factor is the new quality given to space.

So varied, powerful and unhackneyed a medium cannot be forever neglected by the landscape architect. The time will surely come when he will wish to awaken and intensify by his art a consciousness of a garden space at one with that of the house: of the house which is, or should be, only a sequestered part of his garden. Not that space will be his only material of expression: not that gardens are to be built of airy nothings wrapped in cellophane. I would admit to them, in due proportion and relationship, every flower and tree known to gardener, every ornament sculptured or constructed, and every quiet or active pattern of water, provided only that these were consistent with his central intention. But at this moment I am concerned with a principle of unification. Just as in the Renaissance garden this principle is found in the monumental character of the chateau, whose solidity and whose static geometry are repeated in the firm masses of balustraded terraces, steps and clipped foliage, so it may happen that the relation and balance of volumes in the modern house will be transmitted to the garden and re-establish there the ancient unity of house and garden.

I am the more persuaded that such a unity is possible when I consider the importance of space as an æsthetic material in the great traditions of architecture. If the theme of our art is indeed some meaning discovered in the world, if the authority of architecture does indeed arise from its power to reveal the temper of society, what other media is more apposite to this intention than the enclosed spaces which are moulded immediately by the uses and preferences of society? Architecture has always been developed about such spaces. It would be impossible, for example, to imagine the Georgian society in any other theatre than in rooms shaped into prim, geometric forms and balanced decorously along enfilades. We cannot conceive of the seventeenth century except in the oval saloons which melt into each other under sumptuously modelled vaults or along the glamorous progressions of grand stairways. No other medium has received with such candour the imprint of every way of life: the Romanesque space, sombre and inert under the cave-like vaults; the Gothic space, nervous and energetic under membranes of thin stone and amethyst; the Victorian space, fussy and self-conscious and broken into romantic episodes. Not in every instance has the garden echoed the spatial order of the house, but, when this has happened, the splendour of the garden has been immeasurably enhanced by that unity of intention.

Our new space proclaims as eloquently the evolving scheme of our lives, the new patterns of idea and manners, the changed tempo, the wider horizons. Into these new orderings of space there has been translated the grace and order and completeness which the architect has discovered beneath the infinite complexities, the speed, the vast dimensions, and the harsh mechanizations of our world. That which the house tells us, the garden must reaffirm.

BIBLIOGRAPHY

The following is a list of the principal works consulted by the author in the preparation of his manuscript. The books are arranged in chronological order.

Le Notre, André, and others. *Jardins, parterres, portiques, et berceaux de treillage de l'invention des Sieurs Le Nôtre Le Bouteux et Touchar* (Paris, 1680).

Addison, Joseph. *The Tatler*, No. 161 (1710); *The Spectator*, Nos. 412, 414, 477 (1712). *Remarks on the Several Parts of Italy in the Years* 1701, 1702, 1703 (1761).

Pope, Alexander. *The Guardian*, No. 173 (1713).

Switzer, Stephen. *The Nobleman, Gentleman, and Gardener's Recreation* (1715).

Gentil, François, and Liger, Louis. *The Retir'd Gardener, . . .* (translated from the French . . . with several alterations and additions . . . by G. London and H. Wise. Second edition by J. Carpenter, 1717).

Bradley, Richard. *A General Treatise of Husbandry and Gardening* (1726).

Langley, Batty. *New Principles of Gardening* (1728).

Miller, Philip. *The Gardener's Dictionary* (1731-39).

Plan of Mr. Pope's Garden and Grotto, etc. (1745).

Coventry, Francis. *Strictures on the Absurd Novelties introduced in Gardening* (The World, No. 15, April 12, 1753).

Thomson, J. *Works* (two volumes, 1763).

Shenstone, William. *The Works in Verse and Prose of*, Dodsley's Edition (1764-69).

Whateley, Thomas. *Observations on Modern Gardening* (1770).

Chambers, Sir William. *A Dissertation on Oriental Gardening* (1772).

Mason, William. *The English Garden, A Poem in Four Books* (1772-82); *An Heroic Epistle to Sir William Chambers* (1773).

Heely, Joseph. *Letters on the Beauties of Hagley, Envil and the Leasowes* (1777).

Gilpin, William. *Observations . . . relative chiefly to Picturesque Beauty* (eleven volumes, 1783-1809).

Walpole, Horace. *Essay on Modern Gardening* (Strawberry Hill, 1785).

Graves, Richard. *Recollections of some Particulars in the Life of the late William Shenstone, Esq.* (1788).

Promenade ou Itineraire des Jardins d'Ermenonville (Paris, 1788).

Knight, Richard Payne. *The Landscape, a Didactic Poem in Three Books* (1794).

Repton, Humphry. *Sketches and Hints on Landscape Gardening* (1795).

Transactions of the Horticultural Society of London (first series, 1812-30; second series, 1835-48).

Kames, Lord. *Elements of Criticism* (ninth edition, two volumes, 1817).

Spence, Joseph. *Anecdotes, observations and characters, of books and men* (Notes and Life by S. W. Singer, 1820).

Loudon, John Claudius. *The Encyclopædia of Gardening* (1822); *The Landscape Gardening and Landscape Architecture of the late Humphry Repton, Esq.* (1840).

Scott, Sir Walter. *On Ornamental Plantations and Landscape Gardening* (Quarterly Review, 1828).

Johnson, G. W. *A History of English Gardening* (1829).

Floricultural Cabinet, The (edited by Joseph Harrison, 1833-37).

Price, Sir Uvedale. *On the Picturesque, including a Letter to H. Repton, Esq.* (edited by Sir Thomas Dick Lauder, 1842).

Ruskin, John, *Modern Painters* (1843). These volumes contain satiric comments on Italian Landscape in England.

Annals of Horticulture, The (1845-47).

Brayley, Edward Wedlake. *A Topographical History of Surrey* (Volume 2, 1850).

Hibberd, J. Shirley. *Rustic Adornments for Homes of Taste* (1856); *The Amateur's Flower Garden* (1875).

Hughes, John Arthur. *Garden Architecture and Landscape Gardening* (1866).

Mill, John Stuart. *Three Essays in Religion.* 1. *Nature* . . . (1874).

Robinson, William. *The English Flower Garden* (Murray, 1883).

Conder, J. *Landscape Gardening in Japan* (Kelly and Walsh, 1893).

Parker, DeWitt H. *The Analysis of Art* (Yale University Press, New Haven, Conn., 1902).

Ross, Denman W. *A Theory of Pure Design* (Mifflin, New York, 1907).

Lipps, T. *Ästhetik* (1907).

Jekyll, Gertrude. *Colour Schemes for the Flower Garden* (Country Life, 1908).

Ainslie, D. *Æsthetic as Science of Expression* . . . etc. (translated from the Italian of Benedetto Croce, second edition, Macmillan, 1922).

Manwaring, E. W. *Italian Landscape in Eighteenth Century England* (Oxford University Press, New York, 1925).

Le Corbusier and Jeanneret. *Œuvre complète* (volume 1, 1910-29; volume 2, 1929-34).

Le Corbusier. *Towards a New Architecture* (translated by Frederick Etchells. Rodker, 1927); *The City of Tomorrow* (translated by Frederick Etchells. Rodker, 1929).

Wilenski, R. H. *The Modern Movement in Art* (Faber, 1927); *The Meaning of Modern Sculpture* (Faber, 1934).

Hussey, Christopher. *The Picturesque* (Putnams, 1927).

Gothein, Marie Luise. *A History of Garden Art* (translated from the German by Mrs. Archer-Hind. Two volumes, Dent, 1928).

Bean, W. J. *Trees and Shrubs Hardy in the British Isles* (two volumes, 5th edition, Murray, 1929).

Ostwald, Wilhelm. *Colour Science* (translated by J. Scott Taylor). *Part I. Colour Theory and Standards of Colour* (Winsor and Newton, 1931).

Sharp, Thomas H. *Town and Countryside* (Oxford University Press, 1932); *English Panorama* (Dent, 1938).

Bauer, Catherine. *Modern Housing* (George Allen and Unwin, 1934).

Crow, G. H. *William Morris, Designer* (Studio, 1934).

Gwynn, Stephen. *Claude Monet and His Garden* (Country Life, 1934).

Jekyll, Francis. *Gertrude Jekyll, A Memoir* (Cape, 1934).

McGrath, Raymond. *Twentieth Century Houses* (Faber, 1934); *Glass in Architecture and Decoration* (Architectural Press, 1937).

Sartoris, A. *Gli Elementi dell' Architettura Funzionale* (second revised edition, Milan, 1935).

Pevsner, Nikolaus. *Pioneers of the Modern Movement* (Faber, 1936).

Allen, B. Sprague. *Tides in English Taste* (1619-1800) (two volumes, Cambridge, Mass., 1937).

Housing. A European Survey (by the Building Centre Committee. Volume 1, 1937),

Humphreys, A. R. *William Shenstone* (Cambridge University Press, 1937).

Stokes, Adrian. *Colour and Form* (Faber, 1937).

Denby, Elizabeth. *Europe Re-housed* (George Allen and Unwin, 1938).

Mumford, Lewis. *The Culture of Cities* (Secker and Warburg, 1938).

INDEX

All references are to pages of the book. In the case of illustrations the references as well as their page numbers are set in heavy type.